Brat

BRAT

An '80s Story

Andrew McCarthy

GRAND CENTRAL
PUBLISHING

New York   Boston

Grand Central Publishing
Hachette Book Group
1290 Avenue of the Americas, New York, NY 10104
grandcentralpublishing.com
twitter.com/grandcentralpub

First edition: May 2021

Grand Central Publishing is a division of Hachette Book Group, Inc. The Grand Central Publishing name and logo is a trademark of Hachette Book Group, Inc.

The publisher is not responsible for websites (or their content) that are not owned by the publisher.

The Hachette Speakers Bureau provides a wide range of authors for speaking events. To find out more, go to www.hachettespeakersbureau.com or call (866) 376-6591.

Photo credits appear in the back of the book.

Library of Congress Cataloging-in-Publication Data
Names: McCarthy, Andrew, 1962– author.
Title: Brat : an '80s story / Andrew McCarthy.
Description: First edition. | New York : Grand Central Publishing, 2021.
Identifiers: LCCN 2020054051 | ISBN 9781538754276 (hardcover) |
    ISBN 9781538754283 (ebook)
Subjects: LCSH: McCarthy, Andrew, 1962– | Actors—United States—
    Biography. | Motion pictures—United States—History—20th century.
    | Nineteen eighties.
Classification: LCC PN2287.M5446 A3 2021 | DDC 791.4302/8092
    [B]—dc23
LC record available at https://lccn.loc.gov/2020054051

ISBNs: 978-1-5387-5427-6 (hardcover), 978-1-5387-5428-3 (ebook)

Printed in the United States of America

LSC-C

Printing 1, 2021

For Sam, Willow, and Rowan—take care with your youth

Before It

WHEN I BEGAN to consider writing a book about my Brat Pack days, I worried that I wouldn't be able to recall many of the details from so long ago. I wondered if I would need to call upon old friends and work colleagues to fill in the blank spots. Then, as I began to write, things came back. My perspective on some of the more obviously significant moments shifted—certain memories acquired added heft, while others fizzled under the weight of scrutiny. A few "aha" realizations illuminated patterns of behavior I had previously not imagined. Eventually, things strung themselves together into the narrative we have here. In the end, I didn't call upon anyone for their recollections, since what I found myself most interested in was making sense of the version of the past that I have lived with, invested in, and evolved from over the years. What did my story, from my perspective, have to teach me? Groupthink couldn't aid me in that process.

Yet memory can prove unreliable; it can be elusive; it's pliable. Does that mean any attempt at a self-reckoning must be put down as some kind of auto-fiction? Is it all just a semi-true story? Luckily, there are some indisputable facts that can be relied upon. How these things came to pass and how they would influence all that would come after is the subject of this narrative.

What I claim here is not a definitive truth but my experience of the truth, a truth that has informed and shaped my life over the decades. What happened to me during the course of a few brief years, when I came of age within a certain pop culture environment, irretrievably altered who I would become.

Some years ago I wrote a travel book. In truth, it was more a book about coming to terms with my then impending second marriage as I traveled the world far from home. More specifically still, it became a book about how I would come to terms with two very disparate notions that resided firmly inside me—namely, a strong yearning for solitude and an equally strong yet seemingly incompatible desire for a deep and intimate loving connection with another human being. How well I wrestled with these two emotional alligators went a long way in dictating the course of that book (and continues to do so in my marriage).

Only after I was deep into this project did it dawn on me that two seemingly opposing forces had been strongly at play during my youthful success as well. I had a powerful wanting—I might almost call it a vision for myself, except what I was after was something I couldn't quite see but rather a feeling, a knowing, that I experienced when I moved in its direction—coupled with what seemed an equally strong desire to pull away, to hide. It was a familiar yin-yang pattern that probably should have always been obvious to me and yet it wasn't. Perhaps that's because in so many ways I simply ran from my youth. I survived it and wanted to move on. What makes my story any different from others is that mine was a youth that so many might have wished for, myself included. So why run?

This book is an examination of a time that I had willfully ignored for so long—albeit a generation of moviegoers would not always make that easy to do. Sometimes things happen, we live with their result, and then occasionally, a long time distant, we try to make sense of them. The following pages are my attempt to do just that.

Awash in It

MOLLY'S WISDOM TEETH had just been pulled. Cheeks still puffy, she bypassed the red carpet. But she was there. John Hughes was there, too, in a pink sport coat with padded shoulders, a large music clef pin on his wide lapel. His mullet was blow-dried into a flip just above the shoulders. Jon Cryer was happily mugging for the cameras wearing a Western-style string tie, shirt collar turned up. Annie Potts was all smiles. And there were others, celebrities not associated with the movie, eager to be seen at the showbiz event du jour. Cher, Michael J. Fox, a bare-chested George Michael.

Pretty in Pink was my fourth movie and my first Hollywood premiere. I had just been flown in from New York. I was filled with the to-be-expected feelings of excitement as well as a less easily understood sense of dread. It seems probable that one of the studio publicists working the event made sure that someone snapped my photo as I slid along the edge of the red carpet, my eyes on the ground. Yet I'm not aware of a single photo of me from the screening. There were certainly no paparazzi shouting out my name, clamoring for just one more shot.

I had been to Mann's Chinese Theatre before and placed my hands in the cement imprints made by the old-time movie stars in the courtyard out front: Jimmy Stewart's fingers were a little long; however, Steve McQueen's hand fit just right. But I'd never been seated among an audience of a thousand savvy industry types to watch a movie in which I appeared. About two-thirds of the way back in the packed theater, I took a seat as near to the aisle as I could get.

Not long after the lights went down and the opening credits began, I mumbled apologies, climbed over several sets of knees, and darted up the aisle. A few stragglers were getting their free popcorn in the lobby when I pushed open the glass door and lunged out into the cool late-January night. The red carpet, site of such excitement just a short while earlier, was deserted. The velvet ropes that had held dozens of photographers at bay now stood guard over nothing.

Nearby, a few clusters of tourists were laying their hands on the imprints of the immortals, laughing, taking snapshots with clunky flash cameras. At the curb, giant klieg lights still beamed up into the heavens. In my ill-fitting black blazer and skinny tie, I searched up and down Hollywood Boulevard, looking for a place to hide. Directly across the street was Hamburger Hamlet, an old-school Hollywood institution long past its heyday. I hustled by the leather-clad booths and made directly for the deserted bar. Over the next ninety minutes I downed more than a few straight vodkas on the rocks and kept my head down.

Trying

The after-party was at a nightclub called the Palace. Laser lights slashed through the smoky room as that '80s beat filled the air. The club was full. People clustered by the bars, danced; everyone shouted to be heard. I wafted through the party on a cloud of alcohol and cigarettes. Eventually I was corralled, along with James Spader, for a quick on-camera chat. James and I had become close during filming. He was a fellow East Coaster; I felt comfortable with him. For reasons that made sense only in a world created by MTV in the 1980s, Fee Waybill, the lead singer of the Tubes, was conducting interviews and had the unenviable task of trying to get James and me to speak coherently about the movie—or anything at all. James rambled on in his charming, patrician fashion about a car he had once owned. I swayed back and forth, drunk and anxious, blowing cigarette smoke and trying not to appear

3

frozen by the few benign questions that were lobbed my way. In a career of bad interviews, this one was particularly inept. It didn't matter. The movie was about to become a hit—and success would land hard upon me. Over the next several years I would ride high and get tumbled and tossed in the back-wash. What would happen over that brief time would grow to define me in the eyes of a great many—as well as in my own estimation—for a long, long time to come.

Discovering It

AS A NINE-YEAR-OLD fourth grader at Lincoln Elementary School in my hometown of Westfield, New Jersey, I had little theatrical ambition. Not even after I saw the entire sixth grade gather on the stage of the school's gymnasium to perform Three Dog Night's recent hit, "Jeremiah Was a Bullfrog" (more properly known, of course, as "Joy to the World"). My oldest brother, Stephen, was the one in the third row wearing the multicolored bell-bottoms, of which he was rightfully proud. The class sang along to a record, but only their exuberant voices could be heard. They were a smash hit and became instant stars around the water fountain.

All through this year of 1971, I had a wild crush on Dana Crawford. It was my first experience with distracting preoccupation and inexplicable longing, and I kept my feelings secret, especially from Dana. She sat at the desk directly in front of me and I remember staring, transfixed, at the back of her collar-length blond hair from nine to three, five days a week. Naturally, we rarely spoke. But after the sixth graders' show, either Dana or her best friend, whose name is long gone from my memory, decided that our class should get up and sing along to a song at the next assembly.

Most of the details are foggy, but the key facts remain forever in my mind. Instead of the entire class—some twenty-five or thirty kids—getting up to sing, it would be only Dana, her friend, another young boy, and me performing. No auditions were held. No one else wanted to participate. (How did the teacher allow this to move forward?) I can only be sure that the reason I went along was that I would have done anything to get close to Dana. And in that I was lucky. On the day of the big show, we huddled together in the cramped coat closet of our classroom for our one and only rehearsal. I had never been in such close proximity to the object of my affection. I could feel her sweet breath on my face. My nervousness was compounded by the fact that, beyond the classic opening line, I didn't know any of the lyrics to the song we were to sing in front of the entire school in a half hour's time.

Perhaps a little choreography might have helped. Instead, Dana and her friend sat on the edge of the stage, their feet dangling off the front, knee socks pulled up high. The other young boy and I stood in front of them, exposed to the entire school. We were introduced by one of our classmates and I grew incensed when he mentioned the boy who would be spinning the record. What did that kid have to do with our performance? And why spoil the magic by alerting the audience that all the instrumentation and vocals were not ours alone (even though we held no instruments)?

The guitars kicked in. Then so did we—"Yummy, yummy, yummy, I've got love in my tummy." After that I was lost. I mumbled along for a few bars. Soon the others fell silent as well. Only the Ohio Express could be heard, belting it out. I stared at the gymnasium floor for two minutes and twenty-two seconds.

Silence greeted us as we returned to our seats. Mercifully—and for this I will forgive them almost anything—neither of my two older brothers, Stephen or Peter, who must have been in the audience that day, has ever mentioned this humiliation. But the shame of that afternoon still lands on me like a wet towel slapping down on my shoulders whenever I think of it, and the embarrassment I feel all these years later in writing about it is strangely acute. It's a wonder I went on to a career in performing at all.

On a bright afternoon not long after this fiasco, my mother appeared, unannounced, in the doorway of my classroom. I was surprised, then frightened, to see her there. What had happened? But rather than anything being wrong, she had come to liberate me. And she had a plan. We took a bus into New York City, to the recently opened TKTS booth just above Times Square, to buy half-price tickets to see a Broadway show—whatever show had any seats left. I don't know where my mother got such an outlandish idea.

On a few prior occasions she had picked me up after school and taken me—and only me—to a small, deserted amusement arcade out on Route 22. These trips usually coincided with one of the many days when I wept before school, not wanting to leave the safety of home. Young children rarely see their parents as anything beyond an extension of their own lives, yet on these outings I was privy to a loneliness residing in my mother—a loneliness that sprang from her own childhood with an unloving mother and an elderly father— a loneliness usually masked by the busyness of life. We drifted through the arcade in a wash of quiet solidarity.

My mother loved to play Skee-Ball, and together we would roll the wooden ball up the ramp in hopes of scoring a center shot. I don't remember what we were trying to win; it wasn't important. I never saw my mother more unburdened than when she was leaning forward, swinging her arm to send that ball on its way. Memories of those trips to the arcade when I had my mother all to myself are bathed in a warm and melancholy gauze.

But our trip to Broadway was one of pure joy. Tickets procured, we sat down in the front row, center two seats, my mother on my right. I had never been in a Broadway theater before. The lights went to black and the music began. A dozen pairs of hands—seemingly suspended in air—appeared. Caught in a single beam of light cast from one side of the stage to the other, the hands began to move in a strange, mesmerizing pattern. The musical was *Pippin*. The next few hours passed in a hallucinatory whirl of sensory overload. I had never experienced anything remotely like it.

My usual universe consisted of a tight orbit around our home, which sat at the top of a small rise in the center of the block, bound on one end, eight doors down, by the Kings' home and on the other corner by the large gabled house in which, rumor had it, an old woman had died some years earlier and not been discovered for days, maybe even weeks. It was a typical suburban existence now gone, one of absolute afternoon freedom, bike riding and driveway basketball games, the only limitation to be home by six for dinner. Occasionally my mother asked me to look after Justin—my younger sibling by eight years—for a short while during the afternoon. I felt proud to show off my baby brother around the neighborhood, but one day I arrived home solo just in time for dinner. I walked through the door, and my mother asked where Justin was. I froze. At that moment the phone rang: Mrs. Mulholland from across the street was on the line. She had pulled into her driveway and stopped short when she was confronted with an unattended baby stroller. The baby inside looked a lot like ours.

"I was playing hide-and-seek with Julie and Margie." I shrugged. "I forgot."

My mother shook her head: "My little daydreamer." Had it been either Peter or Stephen who misplaced Justin, it's unlikely she would have been so easily forgiving.

Unsurprisingly for a family with four boys, sports were king in my house. Peter was our star, leading his baseball team to the town championship in consecutive years. My skills were not nearly as pronounced, but because I had an older sibling on the team, when I was ten I was "drafted" onto the Athletics. I was quickly deposited out in right field—where the least amount of action could be expected—and left there. This set up a dynamic where I would exist comfortably in Peter's shadow and, more importantly, under his watchful eye throughout our school years.

With Peter, my protector.

My eldest brother Stephen's baseball skills were nearly as modest as mine, and he was quick to abandon his mitt for a set of golf clubs, which better suited his more cerebral temperament.

My father was an umpire around the league. He was famous in town for his low strike zone and his loud, aggressive calling of balls and strikes. A pitch down the center was greeted with a singing "Steeeeee-RIKE!" while an offering off the plate was dismissed with a turn of his head and a digusted bark of "Ball!" Whenever he called a game in which my brother or I was involved, my father went out of his way to be impartial. One afternoon, with my mother in the bleachers holding my little brother in her arms, Peter was at the plate with two strikes. The next pitch bounced in the dirt several feet before home plate. "Steeeee-rike THREE! Yoooooour out!" my father sang as Peter's mouth hung open. My mother shocked us all by letting out a loud and long "Boooo!"

On the occasions when my mother attended my games, I found the pressure too great. After I struck out three consecutive times, I begged her to please stop attending. She agreed, but not before whispering that I should swing at the first pitch each time I was at the plate. "That way," she assured me, "you won't get too nervous being at bat for too long."

Life shifted dramatically in the fifth grade. My brothers and I were transferred from our public schools just down the road to a prep school a half-hour bus ride away in Elizabeth. I don't recall any explanation given by my parents for the move. I was to attend Pingry for the next eight years, until I left for college. I took two things away from my experience there: (1) I was not very smart, and (2) I was going to be an actor. The first realization took me a long time to recover from; the second, I never did.

Initially, my mother insisted that Peter sit beside me on the bus home every day. Near the end of our first week I turned to him and said, "Look, we always get the emergency seat." I nodded toward the small placard below the window instructing that the glass be pushed out from the bottom in case of emergency. Peter stared at me. "They all are," he said, and pointed out the small signs below each of the windows around us. Humiliation crept up my back as I sank low in my seat. I didn't speak until we got home, where I informed my mother I didn't need Peter to sit beside me anymore.

Another equally momentous event centered around the bus a few years later. In seventh grade I was infatuated with Mary Ann Butler. Mary Ann was tall and already quite busty. Aside from my best friend Marston Allen, I was the smallest kid in the class. As such things matter greatly in the seventh grade (and beyond), I was shocked when I got word that Mary Ann liked me as well. For days that felt like weeks, I struggled to summon the nerve to "ask her out"—the parlance for going steady in New Jersey in the 1970s. By Friday afternoon the idea of having to endure another weekend with this monumental task hanging over me was too much. I rushed up to her bus, which, along with ten others, waited out front of school at 3:00 p.m. to scatter kids to their various homes in various towns. Mary Ann lived in tony Short Hills, while my hometown was more modest. She was already seated near the back, but when she saw me rush up to the side of the bus, Mary Ann leaned across the person next to her and stuck her head out the window.

"Do you want to go out with me?" I blurted out.

She shrugged. "Okay."

I called her once over the weekend. Sitting on the edge of my parents' bed while they were downstairs watching TV, Mary Ann and I struggled through a few minutes of conversation. She told me that she was watching a show and I should watch it, too. I replied that my parents were watching something else. There was a pause on the line, then her voice was incredulous: "Don't you have another TV?"

We did not. I wanted to crawl under my parents' bed.

Over the next two weeks I did everything I could to avoid her. I skipped lunch; I feigned a sprained ankle to avoid gym class. At the end of those two weeks I approached Mary Ann at her locker. I had prepared a speech in which I explained how, although I was very fond of her, I thought perhaps we were not an ideal match and it was best if we broke up. When I was finished with my prepared remarks, Mary Ann just looked at me. At last she spoke: "That sounded like a speech."

The names would change, and the details alter, but I would go on to a similar level of success with each of the several girls I fancied throughout my high school years.

As for my academic career, it was over even as it began. Early on, my mother sat with me at the dining room table each evening after dinner, bent over mathematics that neither of us could decipher. By the time I was forced into a special weekly meeting with my adviser, Mr. Baldwin—a terrifying old man with thin and wispy white hair, sharp features, translucent skin, and an unsympathetic manner—I was looked upon as a student who needed extra attention. Perhaps I did, but it was my lack of assertiveness with Mr. Baldwin that fueled his frustration with me. I would spend my entire youth—and years into adulthood—believing that my introverted temperament was a problem, something I had to "get over," "work through," and hopefully "outgrow." My solution as far as school went was to simply disengage and stay as close to the academic periphery as possible. The back-row corner seat quickly became my spot of choice. It remained so for the duration of my education.

The discovery of marijuana in the ninth grade, and my subsequent (and substantial) usage, did nothing to improve my studies.

What caused me significantly more worry than my low grades was the fact that I was late to physically mature. For a brief but intense time I feared there was something biologically wrong with me—that I was missing some inherent gene that I needed to make me a man. On some evenings

I stood in front of the mirror, staring into my baby-faced reflection, wishing—begging—whoever was on the other side of the glass to let me see what I might look like in five years, so afraid was I that I would never mature. I have never understood the appeal of Peter Pan.

With my long hair and high voice, I was often mistaken for a girl. Even more worrisome than my small and delicate stature was something about which I became extremely self-conscious: my lack of manly hair in places other than my head. On the basketball team, in which I was briefly and surprisingly excelling despite my size, I developed a shot where I never raised my arms above my head, so that others would not see my still-bare armpits. It may have been strange to behold, but it was oddly effective.

My father rarely missed a game I played that year of ninth grade, and whenever I scored a basket, he could be heard calling out from the stands, "THAT'S MY BOY!"

His shouts of support humiliated me—which is natural enough for a teenager—but there was something else about his cheers: they rang hollow to me, as if more a performance for the benefit of others than any true expression of pride—something more for him than for me.

My father was a charming, gregarious man, well liked around town and known by name at all the shops. He would chat freely with anyone at any time. Vain about his full head of black hair and long sideburns, his blue eyes invited attention. My father's temper was fearsome in the confines of our four walls, with my oldest brother, Stephen—who never shied from confrontation with our father—often the recipient of the brunt of his aggression. Sitting in the den, watching television one afternoon, I heard them going at each other in the kitchen. I burrowed myself farther down into the couch. A chair scraped hard against the linoleum floor, then Stephen came racing into the den. Without slowing, he made a perfectly judged dive headfirst through the open window and out into the yard, my father in hot pursuit. My dad's anger was usually confined to verbal aggression, but I don't know what might have happened had he caught Stephen on that day. I could never understand my brother's persistent need to confront our father, and I looked on him with a combination of awe and resentment for his constant desire to hit our family's emotional hornet's nest with a stick.

On occasion I would lie in bed and hear my father shouting at my mother downstairs. One night, after a door slam that let me know my father had left the house, I snuck down and discovered my mother crying at the kitchen table. In a rush she wiped her tears and informed me, not for the last time, that children shouldn't see their parents cry.

With me, my father was less overtly aggressive. What I experienced was a more subtle shadow of disregard. So when the film *The Godfather* came out and he began calling me his "consigliere," I was surprised. After he explained to me what the term meant, I was even more shocked. I had never experienced myself as his trusted confidant or adviser. Had I been old enough to see the film, perhaps I would have perceived this new (and short-lived) intimacy as an embodiment of the don's famous advice to "keep your friends close and your enemies closer."

A few years later, when I was an early teen, he took to calling me "Slick." We behaved as if the nickname were an affectionate one and ignored the simmering hostility we both knew it carried. "I love you because I'm your father, but I don't like you," he once hissed at me in disgust. He meant the remark in only transitory anger, but hearing these words—which I experienced like a slap—was an unlikely relief, confirmation of something I had always felt.

My father's rage always put him squarely in the wrong, while my overtly sensitive reactions placed me firmly on the emotional high ground—my mother couldn't help but always take my side. No wonder he disliked me.

But by all accounts, my parents' early years were happy ones. They met when my father, having just returned from his stint in the army, walked into a bakery in Brooklyn. My seventeen-year-old mother was behind the counter. That

Mom (at twenty years old) and Dad, with Stephen.

night she told her parents, "I met the boy I'm going to marry." And at nineteen she did. At twenty she had the first of their four sons. Despite all that would happen between them over the years, my mother still maintains—with a distinct edge but watery-eyed nonetheless—"he was the love of my youth."

One afternoon I missed the three o'clock bus home from school. There would not be another until 5:30 when the sports teams finished practice. I wandered the empty halls. A maintenance man pushed a whirling machine in small circles, buffing the floor. Outside the school chapel, I could hear music coming from within. I cracked the door. There were people busily arranging pieces of a stage set, someone was on a ladder, and there was a cluster gathered around a piano at the base of the stage. The annual school spring musical was being mounted, and loosely controlled chaos was afoot. I slid into the room. Someone walking by told me that the ensemble was running through a few numbers at the piano, I had better hurry up, I was late. I did what I was told and slunk to the periphery of the group huddled around the piano. A red-haired man with a mustache was at the keyboard: Mr. Little, assistant head of the glee club. I had met him a few years earlier, when all seventh graders were forced to try out for the singing group.

Back then my friend Brian Donahue had told me that being a member of the glee club was for losers, so when it came my turn to sing a few scales, I deliberately sang poorly. Mr. Little stopped me after just a few bars and informed me

I was tone-deaf. My services would not be needed in glee club. I was secretly disappointed they didn't want me.

Mr. Little played with passion and leaned hard into his work on the keys. His red hair was thin on top, and he combed it over to make the most of what he had. But when the muse got hold of him he would begin nodding furiously, his hair would flop forward. With lightning speed he'd lift his left hand from the keys, smooth his errant locks back into place, and just as quickly return his fingers to the piano, never missing a note.

On this day Mr. Little did not disappoint, pounding the ivory, lifting his hand to conduct the chorus, his index finger crooked and shaking with passion, hair flying. The ensemble of fifteen or twenty sang through a few songs, and I began to catch on a little to tunes that everyone else knew by heart. No one seemed to notice as I followed the chorus up onto the stage and lurked in the back of the group scenes. I smiled at a few of the ensemble actors around me but spoke to no one. The next day I showed up again.

The drama club was already late in the rehearsal process for a musical called *Hello, Dolly!* about a matchmaking widow to the high society. On the third day I showed up, the cast was buzzing. The show was to begin "tech" rehearsal, when all the pieces—the acting, singing and dancing, lighting, sets and props—were put together onstage for the first time. I would eventually learn that from high school to Broadway the process is roughly the same. Exciting and stressful, tech is when final changes and additions to a show are made, additions that can happen only once everything is put together in those last few days.

It was then that I was plucked from the ensemble and given a small "bit." I thought perhaps Mr. Little had noticed me loitering in the back, remembered my tone-deaf audition for glee club, and suggested to the director that there might be some other way I could contribute besides with my vocal gifts—but there was another reason.

Early in the show Dolly sang a song boasting of her match-making abilities. The number needed some visual aid, and my small stature would finally prove an advantage. As Dolly sang, a very tall girl (a senior named Wendy Wood who later that year would go to the prom with Stephen) and I were instructed to step from the wings and stand side by side, facing the audience. Dolly was to sashay over to us, place her hands on my hips, and hop me closer to my statuesque partner. Wendy was told to bend down, scoop me up, and carry me offstage like a bundle. That was it.

Opening night arrived and I stood nervously in the wings as Mr. Little pounded the first bars of our song. Dolly strutted toward our side of the stage. Wendy and I were nudged out. We stood awkwardly facing the audience as instructed. Dolly scooted me a bit closer to Wendy, who promptly snatched me up, just as we had rehearsed the day before.

It was then that theatrical inspiration visited me for the first time. As Wendy was carrying me off the stage, without fore-thought, I reached up and planted a kiss on her cheek. Wendy smiled a wide and warm grin, and the audience laughed and clapped their approval.

The director was waiting for me in the wings and bent down to get in my face—"What did you do?"

"I'm sorry," I whispered back, my shoulders rising.

"That was fantastic!"

I had misunderstood his nervous energy. My spirits soared. After the show, others commented as well and congratulated me on my impulsive action.

The following night—which happened to be closing night—I stood beside Wendy in the wings again, feeling less nervous as Mr. Little struck up those first few notes. Wendy and I went out on cue. Dolly sauntered over. She hopped me closer to my very tall partner. Wendy lifted me up like crepe paper and began to carry me off…and I did nothing. For some reason I held back. As we exited the stage Wendy didn't smile and there was no laughter or applause from the audience.

Following impulses is something you hear about the first day in acting school—and every day thereafter. Freely responding to and allowing unplanned urges is one of the keys to success. Students and professionals alike spend a great deal of their time working to cultivate an atmosphere of spontaneity. Its presence can enliven a situation that otherwise might lie flat—my impromptu kiss had proven that. Unwittingly, I had learned my first major acting lesson.

If I had to guess why I didn't kiss Wendy that second night, I might attribute it to an offhanded comment Peter had made earlier that day. I was no doubt pleased with myself over my sudden and surprising success. In savoring my moment I had stepped out of my lane. Peter quickly put me back in my place the way only a sibling can: "You think you're cool now because you kissed a senior on the cheek?"

His comment had been in passing, just a reaction to my taking up more space than was normal, but because I so admired my older brother, what I heard was a reprimand that cut deep.

In my first brief showbiz outing I had experienced the fickle nature of public adulation, the personal disappointment of stifled creativity, and familial resentment. I considered my theatrical career over.

The following year I was cut from the basketball team—after just one shining season. At fifteen and still the smallest kid in the class, I was washed-up. Drifting through my afternoons now, it was my mother, while preparing dinner, who suggested I try out for the spring musical.

"I don't want to be in a stupid play," I told her. "I want to be the point guard."

"You're too short," Peter chimed in as he passed through the kitchen.

The production was *Oliver!* (exclamation point theirs), a musical adaptation of the Charles Dickens novel *Oliver Twist*. Set in Victorian London, *Oliver!* tells the story of a young orphan who finds his way into a street gang led by a sinister father figure, Fagin. The part I set my sights on was Fagin's first lieutenant, a charming young ne'er-do-well pickpocket known as the Artful Dodger, who takes Oliver under his wing.

I had one problem: Mr. Little.

Now, I was not remotely blessed with a singer's voice. As small children, all three of my kids asked me to please, please stop singing them lullabies at bedtime; my daughter was never shy about putting her fingers in her ears. But I was never as bad as I had led Mr. Little to believe.

It was obvious that he preferred a tall, handsome, cherub-voiced classmate of mine for the role. A competitive streak of which I was previously unaware surfaced in me.

"He's a kiss-ass," I complained to my mother over dinner.

"Well, then it wouldn't hurt you to be a little nicer, either."

Peter confirmed my assessment. "The kid's a dick."

After the first round of auditions Mr. Little regarded me with overt skepticism and he called me in for a private consultation. His basement office was large enough to accommodate an upright piano, its bench, and a few square feet for a singer to stand. He led me through the same scales I had sung during my glee club tryout a few years earlier. Then I sang "Consider Yourself," the Artful Dodger's trademark song. Afterward I was dismissed without comment.

At the final audition, my taller, more handsome, better-voiced competitor and I stood side by side, alternating reading the lines, then singing the songs, one after the other. The prettier he sang, the harder I leaned into my homemade Cockney accent.

There had been few opportunities in my young life up to then—usually associated with sports—when I had been asked to step up and meet an opportunity, to demonstrate both desire and ability in a single moment. I had always shied from such a challenge. Perhaps intimidated by my brothers' successes, I had always believed myself insufficient, or was simply too fearful to risk much. But on this day I went toward what I wanted in a way that had no precedent in my life. I recall no conscious decision to do so, only that I found myself fully extended, engaged, and committed in a way I had never been before, without the luxury of self-doubt. I had leapt—or been pushed by some internal force of which I had been previously unaware—without regard for where I might land. Only the leaping mattered. And in leaping, I landed in myself.

My first playbill.

When speaking about love, Blanche DuBois in Tennessee Williams's *A Streetcar Named Desire* says, "It was like you suddenly turned a blinding light on something that had always been half in shadow." I have no better way to describe the feeling that came over me when I stepped onstage as the Artful Dodger. In hiding behind torn pants and a top hat, I was liberated. I suddenly made sense to myself.

It is, of course, easier to untangle events and see their significance in hindsight, but I knew enough to realize that whatever had happened to me on that stage was important. Yet I told no one the magnitude of my new feelings. If, as Tennessee Williams had written, a light had been turned on, then mine was a single candle's flame, one I knew might be easily extinguished.

My mother's attitude toward my newfound theatrical impulses was one of pleasant support, while my father chose to ignore what he couldn't understand. Stephen had by now gone off to college, Justin was too young to have an opinion on the matter, and Peter's attitude was simply "It's just Andy doing what Andy does." His casual approval went a long way toward confirming the decision that was forming in me.

The following year, when I announced to my parents that

My finest performance.

I intended to study acting in college, my father was quick to snap, "No son of mine is going to be a fucking thespian." But by then my desire had taken deeper root. I was going to do what I was going to do. Though I was standing across the table from them on the screened-in porch, my dad went on as if I weren't there. "He may seem sensitive, but that kid's got steel in him."

I took this as a compliment my father very much did not intend. But what my dad could apparently see that others, including myself, could not fully identify at this point was a drive toward what I could imagine for myself, something that was mine alone. Up to this point, that drive simply had yet to find a focus.

I had two things in my favor to counter my father's resistance to my choice of study. First, my grades in high school were so bad that it was unlikely I would have gotten into a decent college based on my academic transcript alone. Second, my mother was always sensitive to my inner life. I'm not sure how much she understood what it was I was trying to do—how could she when I understood so little?—but she could sense the intensity of my yearning. Eavesdropping from the top of the stairs, I heard my mother stand up to my father in a voice she rarely summoned: "If that's what he wants to do, then we are going to support him in doing it." My father quickly lost interest in this battle. (After starring in my first film opposite Jacqueline Bisset, my father insisted he had been a strong advocate of my acting from the start and urged me to invite Jackie home for dinner. I did not.)

My discovery of acting also paid more immediate dividends. Instead of solely being Stephen and Peter's little brother, suddenly I had carved out my own niche. No one in my family had ever had anything to do with acting, the theater, or show people. This belonged to me and was beyond anyone else's reach. I developed a few friendships with other kids who did plays at school but felt little affinity with the theater/music clique. I was comfortable to stand on my own, existing in my own internal micro-stratum, engaged but separate. And since I now had my feet under me, I wasn't motivated by the need for external validation and was able to cross social boundaries with impunity and in accordance with my own desires.

New York City in the late 1970s was just a few years removed from President Gerald Ford declining to bail the five boroughs out of a fiscal crisis, prompting the famous *Daily News* headline "FORD TO CITY: DROP DEAD." The memory of the blackout, which caused large-scale looting and highlighted racial tensions, was still fresh. And Mayor Koch was asking anyone who would listen, "How'm I doing?"

"Lousy" was how my father always characterized his efforts.

All of this was lost on me as I made my way, five days a week for six weeks, from my rural New Jersey home to the city to attend a summer acting program the year after my life-altering turn as the Artful Dodger. It was my slightly oddball friend Jon Pasternak—with whom I smoked too much pot and endured too many Grateful Dead bootleg albums—who had found out about the classes. Together we navigated the train into Hoboken, the PATH under the Hudson River, and the number 1 subway up to Seventy-Second Street.

Perhaps the most dangerous part of our commute was the one block we walked from the subway to the Ansonia hotel, where the school was located. Verdi Square, a small triangle of land where Broadway crosses Amsterdam Avenue above Seventy-Second Street, was known by local drug users as "Needle Park," immortalized as such in an early Al Pacino movie.

"How are our parents letting us do this?" I asked Jon one day after watching someone shoot up on a nearby park bench.

"Fuck if I know," Jon replied, eyes wide.

While I learned little about acting in that summer session, the experience allowed me to quickly discover *where* I wanted to be. New York was graffiti-scarred, smelly, exhilarating.

It was a hot, heady summer. I ate alone in a restaurant for the first time, was propositioned by my first prostitute, and was swindled out of all my money in a game of three-card monte. Played on the street, atop a cardboard box, by fast-talking, lightning-fingered con men, three-card monte was a 1970s urban version of the old shell game. A player tried to locate the red "money" card among the other two black cards as the dealer shifted them around, facedown, at a brisk pace. A shill, planted in the crowd, won game after game, collecting gobs of what appeared to be easy money, while the mark watched until he had gathered enough courage to play for himself—at which point the mark placed his twenty-dollar bill on the cardboard box and pointed out what was sure to be the red card, only to find the black one.

Was it simply that Jon was absent on this day and I had no restraining force upon me? After watching a dozen hands, guessing correctly in my mind every single time, I stepped forward through the small crowd and slapped down twenty dollars. Then I lost again—my entire week's travel and food allowance in less than sixty seconds. My attempt to ask for my money back was met with hostile derision that sent me fleeing. I stood outside the subway until I had begged enough money to get home.

Not long after this, another valuable lesson offered itself up to me.

I did another play at school and was miscast in a small part with just one major scene. My scene partner was a dapper classmate named Andre LeLong. In his daily life around campus, Andre slicked back his hair, wore a three-piece suit, and carried a walking stick. He sported a pocket watch and monocle. By senior year he was even able to grow a wispy mustache to complete the look. He was deeply odd, and I liked him. But occasionally, during rehearsal, Andre inverted two lines that irretrievably took us to the end of the scene.

The lines in question were not dissimilar, so it was an understandable and easy mistake to make, yet it was an error that excised nearly my entire role. As rehearsals progressed, Andre's occasional miscue grew to be a constant flub—one that would cause us to stop, go back, and correct. But there would be no stopping in front of an audience.

Opening night arrived. My friend Jon, who had the lead role in the play, invited me to take a few hits off a joint before the show. While it seemed to relax him, I quickly regretted the move—fear and paranoia raced in and I sweated out most of my high before the curtain. As I stood in the wings next to Andre, I drilled the correct cue into his ear over and over again. Each time he whispered back the same mistake, shook his head, apologized, and tried again.

The lights went up and we made our entrance. I offered my line and Andre spun on me, arched his well-made-up brow, and delivered the correct cue line to me.

I had no response.

Andre stared at me, brow still arched, waiting. I began to stumble around the stage, stammering, desperately reaching for my lines, which were nowhere to be located in my now panicking, half-stoned brain. This went on for what seemed an eternity until Jon, waving his arms frantically in an attempt to get my attention and stop my blithering, was somehow able to get us back on track enough to get me off the stage.

My show business takeaway: mind your own fucking business.

The mistake I made was not unlike an error that I later began noticing while making movies and continue to see as a television director. Often, for any number of reasons, one of the two players in a given scene is more "in the zone" than the other. Occasionally the scene flounders because of this imbalance. The actor who is on top of his game will often notice the scene not going well and will overwork, trying to force the action. It's never successful. Invariably, the other actor comes off looking relaxed and capable, while the actor who tries to carry more than his share of the burden appears strained and off balance.

It's a problem that's easily solved but perhaps counterintuitive. Let it fail. It's what someone once said to me and, when directing, what I have quietly whispered to actors. "It's not your responsibility to make this scene work. Just play your part. If the scene fails, let it fail. It's my problem." The relief that invariably crosses the actor's face is palpable.

My classmates were applying to multiple colleges throughout the Northeast, down south, and in the Midwest. Most had visited campuses, attended homecoming weekends, written letters, and sought out contacts. I had not.

I'm not sure what I was thinking or why my parents hadn't encouraged me to visit schools as my brothers had done. Perhaps it was simply that I was the third child to go through the process and they had fatigued. I certainly never pushed the point.

I applied to two schools. I knew nothing about either place except that they were located in the city where I knew I wanted to be, and that one, New York University, had a drama program that required an audition.

I needed a monologue. None of the four plays I appeared in during high school had anything approaching a two-minute speech that I might use. And I had never read another play. I knew the names of no playwrights, nor did I know what kind of material might be suitable.

Since I had discovered in acting something that I believed was so important to me, it would be normal to assume that I might have spent some time learning what I could about it. It simply wasn't the case. Acting, once discovered, was just something I was going to do—as if the decision alone were enough and the rest would fall into place. Add to that, somewhere in a private corner of my mind was a notion that I would attend college for two years and then leave school to become a professional actor. How any of this might happen, I had no idea.

But first I needed to get into a college that I could drop out of.

I had a friend named Liz with whom I used to smoke pot most days after school, and Liz's mother was the choreographer for the school musicals. One afternoon, while smoking a large bowl of Mexican gold together, I mentioned my problem to Liz. A few days later she handed me a thin book of actor monologues, courtesy of her mother.

Near the beginning of the collection, one speech got my

attention. I liked the first line: "You know what the most beautiful two words are in the entire English language? Cellar door." Since I didn't read the play (it didn't occur to me), I had absolutely no context for what the character was talking about. I would tell you now, but I never did get around to reading the play and still have no idea. But what I intuitively understood was that it demonstrated an off-center voice and a provocative, pseudo-sexual engagement with the audience. I knew I would get the listener's attention. I just had to keep it for two minutes.

The man whose attention I needed to retain was a petite, bow-tied dandy with a waxed mustache. Fred Gorelick sat behind a folding table in a room that was painted entirely black, something I would later learn was called a black box theatre—painted to create a neutral environment for any variety of things to be performed in it. I entered into that room and, for a second time in my life, I leapt.

When I finished my monologue about the cellar door, Mr. Gorelick asked me if I had something else I could show him. Stumped for an alternative, I offered to perform a few lines from my ace in the hole, the Artful Dodger.

I not only recited the lines but began to strut around the stage, stepping high, lifting my feet as if pulling them up out of one deep bucket and placing them down in another. Why I did this, I have no idea.

Mr. Gorelick asked me to sit down. As he fiddled with his mustache, the small man across the table quizzed me on why my grades were so bad. I shrugged a few times.

"Do you want to act?" he asked me.

"I do," I swore to him.

He nodded in silence, still fingering his mustache. Then he decided to change my life. We made a deal. He would get me into the school if he could, and I promised to maintain a B average. He was sure I would be placed on academic probation to start—one slip and I was out. I nodded vigorously. No problem.

It was a wet spring, and my high school graduation was held inside the chapel. When I heard my name called, I stepped up and walked across the same stage where I had performed in my various plays. The school headmaster, Mr. Cunningham, had taught me for a trimester of my senior year—an English class I only sporadically attended. Regardless, we had a cordial relationship. He smiled as I approached. He was a tall man, well over six feet. He held out my diploma. (Peter had assured me that the ink on it would still be wet.) As I neared, Mr. Cunningham extended his hand to me and leaned down close to my ear. He whispered, "Go get 'em, Dodger."

The Edge of It

ON A TUESDAY morning in the autumn of 1980, I was sitting high up in the back of a windowless lecture hall off Washington Square Park in Greenwich Village. The man at the podium down front had an unruly mop of dark hair and a casually disheveled corduroy look about him. His name was Mel Gordon. My freshman theater history teacher at NYU, he was lecturing about the '60s and '70s: hippies, Vietnam, Watergate—things that made those decades specific and meaningful. What this had to do with theater, I couldn't readily follow. But then he said something, a meaningless, throwaway line that probably wasn't even a part of his lecture.

"And the eighties," Mel said—here he paused to reach up and push back his floppy hair before continuing, "the eighties haven't started yet." At which point he went on with his lecture, of which I remember nothing more.

What was it that made me hear this aside in such a way that it would stay with me for even five minutes, let alone all these years? Did I register some kind of challenge in his words, or see opportunity? Surely my thinking was not so grand.

During an orientation meeting around this same time, a professor announced to a full auditorium, "No one here knows who you were before. You are free to reinvent yourself. You can be anyone you want to be." A buzz went through the vast room. It seemed that, to many in attendance, this permission was what they had been waiting for. Although I'd already started to develop a mask of aloof detachment that bought me some distance from the acute fear I felt in many situations—as well as protection for the desires that were fermenting in me—I wasn't yearning to escape into some new version of myself (if I could even come up with one). At seventeen, I just wanted my life to begin.

Because my family lived so close to the city, and because NYU had limited space, I was not offered housing in any of the dorms. So my father did the kind of headline-grabbing stunt he did best and drove with me in tow into New York City shortly before school began. Stomping the streets of Greenwich Village, he went door-to-door, chatting, charming, asking anyone who would listen if they knew of an apartment for rent, while I hurried along in his shadow. Within a few hours he had found a small one-bedroom, four flights up in a town house, a half block off Washington Square Park. My landlord was a therapist who saw patients in his parlor-floor office. When I observed that he seemed like a nice man, my father assured me, "Shrinks are all crazy."

My rent was a staggering $725 per month, far more than what a dorm would have cost. I put a note on a school bulletin board; a graduate law student with a ready smile and thinning hair knocked on my door. After giving my apartment the once-over, David informed me that he would be my roommate. He occupied the tiny bedroom while I slept in the cramped main room behind a bamboo curtain. We rarely saw each other. Early each morning I heard him whistling in the bathroom; soon after, the apartment door opened and then quietly closed. I'd then stumble to the shower, pluck David's hair from the drain, and start my day.

Washington Square Park became my living room. In 1980 the park was still a hive of post-bohemian cross-culture. My apartment was just off the west side, where hard-edged intellectuals played speed chess and soccer-playing Rastafarians sold loose joints. The east side of the park, where many of my classes were located, was a haven for the elderly sitting on benches and classical musicians with violin cases lying open to collect coins. The center of the park, around the fountain, was a free-for-all where kids with guitars still tried to be the next Leonard Cohen, students swarmed, and a comedian named Charlie Barnett held sway most afternoons. Charlie had a certain unwashed appeal. His voice could carry, his hands were expressive, and he could hold a good-size crowd around the fountain. He spoke the language of the street that I hadn't heard before. Charlie never knew of my existence, but for a new kid in town he almost felt like a friend. (I wasn't the only one to notice Charlie, he eventually went on to appear in a few films and TV shows before suffering an early death.)

Most afternoons, when my classes were over, I would loiter in the park. I'd take in Charlie's act if he was around, then buy two joints for a dollar each from the same Rastafarian every time and head home to watch *The Rockford Files.* I was lonely, always a little scared, and happy.

And I began to learn how to act.

NYU had affiliated itself with various acting schools around the city and farmed its students out. I spent Monday, Wednesday, and Friday buying tokens and riding the subway up to Midtown to Circle in the Square Theatre School. Tuesday and Thursday I'd occasionally drop into my academic classes around Washington Square. I had even less interest in books and chalkboards than I had had during high school. But the strange new world of theater people I suddenly found myself in was quietly thrilling.

What I had experienced back in high school as a flash feeling, some kind of abstract connection to myself—one that I thought no one else could understand—these people assumed as a common starting point. They had all experienced, in one manner or another, their version of that white-light experience I had when I walked onstage in *Oliver!* They approached the cultivation of it as a vocation.

The teachers took the work of play seriously and let it be known that a steep climb lay ahead for anyone who wished to undertake it. Since I had never met any professional associated with the theater or acting, their varying attitudes offered a quick case study in the long-term effects of a commitment to show business and taught me nearly as much as their prepared lessons. I encountered passion, bitterness, delight, fatigue, playfulness, envy, discipline, resentment, professionalism, slapdash habits, highly honed skills, varying degrees of commitment to the students, and nearly always a deep dedication to the work and their relationship to it. They were lifers.

Just trying to follow along...

...and messing around in between.

Leaving any question of talent aside, I had never committed to any form of active learning and was daunted by the
kind of grit they were demanding. I had no experience of
it. If I was going to get along, I would first need to learn
how to learn.

There were classes in acting technique (what was that?),
voice and speech (there was a difference?), modern and jazz
dance (I was not going to tell my father I was taking *dance*—
talk about thespians!). And there was a class in which we
performed scenes from plays; that at least seemed straight-
forward enough.

Yet it was in that scene study class that I got my first slap
down. It came at the hands of a small, olive-skinned Greek
man with silver hair. Nikos Psacharopoulos had an outsize personality and reputation. He had founded the famed
Williamstown Theater Festival, taught at Yale, and was feared
by students. The first day of class, he stood before us and
demanded that we call out the names of plays from which
we might prepare and perform a scene for his inspection.
Students began to bark out titles. Like Caesar giving the
thumbs-up or thumbs-down, Nikos passed instant judgment
as to whether a student was suitable for a particular play by
using his thick, nasal Greek accent—"Ye" or "Ne." He rejected
most offerings. The class grew more and more frenzied as they
hungered for his approval. The titles came faster, students
overriding each other, shouting. There seemed to be no title
that Nikos didn't know.

Those students whose choices were approved sat back with
smug satisfaction. Having never read a play, I had no titles I
could suggest and hid in the back of the class. A few weeks

later, when I was the only one who had still not selected a play, a classmate suggested I do a scene from a nineteenth-century Henrik Ibsen play called *Peer Gynt*. I had never heard of it. I called the title out. Nikos shrugged and snapped, "Ye."

I chose the first scene in the play and never read the rest— after all, it was in five acts and very long. And translated from Danish, it seemed pretty boring. When I finally got up to perform the scene with my partner, Nikos stopped us after only a few lines.

"Eeeh, what are you doing?" he snapped, his harsh, high-pitched voice more nasal than usual.

"Um, what do you mean?" I asked.

"Why are you jumping around the stage and falling over? And what the hell are you doing, picking up your feet like that? Sit down."

As I moved past him on the way back to my seat, the small Greek man hissed—"Eeeh, you have no talent. You should not waste my time. Do something else with your life."

To all appearances, his comment had no effect on me. I kept my eyes on the floor and found my seat in the back. Class ended and I slouched into the hall. Bypassing the others waiting for the elevator, I made for the back stairs. One landing down, a gentle doe-eyed girl who would go on to play a much larger role in my life called after me. Feeling caught, I stopped. She hurried down the flight of steps and whispered, "When you fell on the ground during the scene, the whole floor shook, there was so much energy." I nodded and moved off, unable to convey to her, or anyone, the disappointment and sense of isolation I was experiencing. I never forgot Carol's generosity in that instant when I felt so lost.

But I never did another scene in Nikos's class. He died in 1989, never having had the opportunity to see my subtle and nuanced work in *Weekend at Bernie's II.*

I struggled in other classes as well. I had speech class with a small, prim man named Rick Ericson. Rick (we called all our professors by their first names) quickly developed an attitude of permanent disappointment in me. This may have been because I had no idea what I was doing, or perhaps because my defenses led me to behave as if I just didn't care.

But in this case, maybe I didn't care all that much. The class focused primarily on Shakespeare, and I was quick to realize I would never be a Shakespearean actor. I just could not see its relevance. While the words were no doubt beautiful (or so everyone said), I found it difficult to extract precise meaning from them, and felt I lacked the authority needed to carry them off. The class elicited the same feelings of anxiety and dread in me that academia had.

For someone who loved the verse as Rick did, it must have been painful to listen to a student like me butcher the iambic pentameter, despite his clapping along to try to keep me in time. He often appeared to be physically suffering whenever I garbled my way through the twenty-ninth sonnet.

But it only takes one.

And that one, for me, was a teacher named Terry Hayden. While just in her early sixties at the time, to a seventeen-year-old kid, Terry seemed ancient. Her hair had gone white, she shuffled slowly along with a cane, and she always carried a small footstool in a mesh bag. Her vaguely southern accent wafted with a quiver. She could be charming and then snap like a snake. She was wildly insightful and often dismissed as crazy by teachers and students alike.

Terry: my teacher.

She saved me.

Circle in the Square Theatre School didn't seem to have an overarching philosophy that I could detect, but several of the teachers, primarily Terry, were versed in "the Method."

The Method is the most widely misunderstood (and maligned) school of acting I know. The term itself has grown to become the eye-rolling go-to word to describe self-indulgent, erratic actor behavior. The reality of what the Method has to offer is very different. Based on Russian actor and director Konstantin Stanislavski's series of rehearsal exercises that he

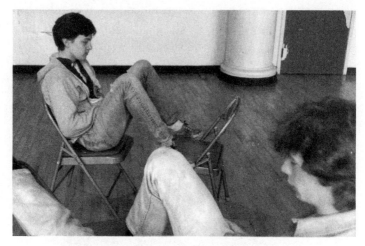

Learning "the Method."

called "the system," the Method that we most commonly think of today is largely the result of American acting teacher Lee Strasberg. Strasberg's interpretation of Stanislavski's work evolved into a series of specific exercises that delve into the personal experiences of the actor in order to elicit authentic emotion and unconscious behavior that might illuminate a given character.

Strasberg rose to prominence in the mid-twentieth century along with the Actors Studio on West Forty-Fourth Street in Hell's Kitchen. Actors such as Marlon Brando, Paul Newman, and Al Pacino are all famously associated with the Method (although Brando studied with Stella Adler, whose approach to the Method differed from Strasberg's).

Terry was a member of the Actors Studio and a disciple of Strasberg, whom she considered a flawed genius. Her interpretation of his work took things a step further—even deeper into the personal, delving into family dynamics and history. On the first day our class met, we began with what Terry called a "sound exercise" (a variation of Strasberg's "song exercise"), in which the actor stands in front of the class and sings the first song that pops into his or her head, singing just one syllable at a time; for instance, Happy Birthday would be sung—"HAAAAAA," deep breath, "PEEEEEEEE," and so on. Despite the simplicity, it can be a raw, unnerving experience, one that exposes a lot about the participant and his or her vulnerabilities and defenses.

With effort, Terry turned in her chair at the front of the class and peered around. I thought I was well hidden in the back behind someone's head. Apparently, I wasn't. Up I shuffled to the front of the class. She explained the exercise and the first song that popped into my head was, unsurprisingly, "Consider Yourself" from my *Oliver!* days.

Maybe because I misunderstood that I was supposed to stay rooted in one place, or perhaps because I had no awareness of what my limbs and torso were doing, I was not able to stand still. After I had gotten through a dozen isolated syllables of the song, Terry asked me to sing it in full, as was customary for the exercise. That's when I really started jumping around, even adding choreography from my high school production. But unlike Nikos (and others), Terry saw my "bucket walk" for what it was: the electric current of life finally getting its chance to be expressed, however amateurishly, forcing itself through me so powerfully that I was as yet unable to contain it.

The degree to which I was unable to control my energy while performing equaled the degree to which I was learning to hide my true reactions when I wasn't. By the time Terry tilted her head to the side, squinted at me, and suggested that I might yet be "too young to do the work," I was already nodding in that nonchalant way, displaying indifference and disregard, masking the disappointment and hurt that I had already accepted as normal in all school circumstances. But then Terry surprised me by adding, "But I think you might want to stick around."

I stopped moving. I had just been plucked from the doesn't-have-what-it-takes-and-doesn't-know-how-to-work role that I had allowed myself to be cast in and, for the moment at least, had potential. I felt seen for the first time by a professional.

My habitual nonchalance was no match for the wide grin that spread across my face. As I went to sit down, Terry left me with one of her prophetic double-edged zingers, one that seemed to contain more insight than could possibly have been available to her after such a brief, initial encounter: "And if you keep smiling like that, you're going to charm us all, and it will be your downfall."

My life outside of school was a small one. I often ate dinner with classmates in the nearby dorm, then drifted home by various indirect routes. It was during these rambles that I began to develop the New Yorker's love of walking the street. I smoked pot and threw the Frisbee in Washington Square with my friend Mickey, a funny freethinker from Pingry who had skipped college altogether and moved nearby. And I was beginning to form a friendship with a former high school teacher of mine.

Eddie was from Texas. Shortly after his graduation from Columbia, he had come to Pingry to teach English. I took his class for a trimester during my senior year. Perhaps because of his relative youth in comparison to the other teachers, or that he spoke to us as peers and hinted at a more exciting life outside of school, I felt an immediate affinity toward him. In a move that was uncharacteristically bold for me, I looked him up when I came into the city. To my surprise, Eddie welcomed me into his world. He threw me into the mosh pit at the Beacon Theater when the B-52's unveiled their latest single, "Private Idaho," and dragged me into CBGB to bang heads as hard punk took it over. In time we'd frequent the downtown clubs like the Limelight and Area beside the Holland Tunnel.

Eddie shopped in the secondhand clothing stores that were ubiquitous in Greenwich Village. He wore baggy olive drab army fatigues a decade before I saw anyone else wear them, which he complemented with a vintage suit jacket. In the winter he added a long camel-hair overcoat. I began to scour the shops on Eighth Street. I had the misguided notion that if I bought the already baggy clothes a size or two even larger, then my slight frame would gain some stature. They felt like the suit of armor I'd been searching for, and I slouched around the Village with more confidence. When winter hit, I added the oversize camel-hair overcoat as well.

In a few years' time, I would model my wardrobe for *St. Elmo's Fire* on this style. The director, Joel Schumacher, who had been a window dresser and later a wardrobe designer himself, liked the eclectic juxtaposition of the fatigues and blazer and loved the overcoat but drew the line at the massively oversize cut.

I would mine Eddie's fashion instincts for wardrobe throughout my '80s films. He occasionally wore a pair of bowling shoes that he had quietly procured when I was with him late one night at Bowlmor Lanes (now gone) on University Place off Union Square. I stole this idea for *Mannequin*, wearing bowling shoes throughout the movie. And the retro suits with narrow lapels and skinny ties I wore in *Less Than Zero* flew directly in the face of '80s fashion and were right out of Eddie's teacher closet. But my ultimate homage to Eddie was in *Weekend at Bernie's*. Not only did I mimic Eddie's summer-in-the-city long, baggy shorts, Hawaiian shirts, and purple Keds high-tops, but my character was entirely based on how I thought Eddie might react to every situation if he were to never once use his brain.

When Eddie's small Yamaha motorcycle was running, I'd climb on the back and we'd head downtown to some of the less trodden dive bars of the Financial District. There was little life far below Canal Street after dark. I turned eighteen years old that fall, I looked twelve, and was never asked for ID at any pub we walked into; such was New York City in the early 1980s. We sat at the bar of the Raccoon Lodge or Puffy's Tavern and debated the merits of Elvis Costello's wordplay, or whether the Clash's *London Calling* was more relevant than Lou Reed's *Street Hassle*.

On a few occasions, I fell off the back of Eddie's bike. But as it was a bad machine and could never get up much speed, and I was usually quite drunk when this happened, no real damage ever occurred. Closer to home, Eddie introduced me to the Corner Bistro, where I settled in and began to lay the foundation for a way of drinking that would develop, to quote Shakespeare, "as if increase of appetite had grown / by what it fed on," and would in several years cause me no end of trouble.

The Bistro is now a fairly well-scrubbed institution attracting tourists for hamburgers that make many "ten best" lists, but back then it was just a local West Village dive bar: wooden, dark, safe. I was young and searching for a way to navigate through the world. Those evenings with Eddie seemed like a way forward. When my brother Peter had gone off to college a few years earlier, the sudden absence of his protective presence had left a void. With Eddie, I felt looked after again in a way I didn't realize I'd craved since my brother's departure.

The damage to this photo perfectly matches the hangover Eddie and I had here.

On Halloween that first year in the city I threw a party. This seemingly trivial event is notable for two reasons. It was the first and perhaps the last party I ever threw, and second, I lost my virginity that night—sort of.

In high school, there had been a few make-out sessions and one girl who was eager to go all the way, save for the fact that I just couldn't "find it" and didn't know that I was allowed to use my hands to help guide things along. And there had been one girl recently, in my freshman acting classes, with whom I had rolled around on my bed one afternoon. But sex with other people was simply not, despite my yearnings, a very active part of my life as of yet.

The party was a huge success. The music was loud and my apartment overflowed. Classmates—people I knew and others I didn't recognize—brought friends and friends of friends. The crowd surged and flowed as people came and went. As the night wore down, the party grew quiet and a young woman I had never seen before asked me for a beer. Then everyone else was gone and we were alone. With little formality, this young woman whose name I'm not sure I ever learned, rolled down the bamboo curtain beside my bed. Thankfully, she seemed to know what to do. Soon she was straddling me. As things began to find their way, she abruptly stopped moving and, looking down at me, asked, "Are you Asian?"

It seemed an odd question at that moment.

"Um, no," I said.

"Are you sure?" she asked.

"I don't think so," I answered.

She went back to business but kept looking down at my chest in a strange way. I was beginning to get more uncomfortable than I already had been—which is saying a lot.

Then she stopped again.

"Are you sure you're not Japanese or something?"

"Why do you keep asking me that?" I blurted out. "Is there something wrong with my dick?"

"Your cock is nice but you don't have very much body hair, and Asians don't have much body hair, so I thought maybe you were Japanese or Chinese."

"I'm pretty sure that I'm definitely not," I said, but really I wasn't sure of anything anymore. "Do you want to use some Vaseline?" I asked.

I'd heard somewhere that Vaseline (which I had beside my bed for my dry hands) was a good sex aid and I wanted to show her that I knew what I was doing.

"Sure," she replied.

We kept at it for a bit longer, and then the whole thing just sort of stopped before either of us really got anywhere and she was up and gone. Never to be seen or heard from again. For some time after, this unfulfilled act was the highlight of my sex life.

Not long before midnight on December 8, during that first year in New York, I was in my apartment, having just smoked a joint. Flipping the dial on my Pioneer receiver, I tuned in, as I usually did at that time of the night, to WNEW.

Back in New Jersey, my brother Stephen had exposed me to a smoky-voiced radio DJ named Alison Steele, aka "the Nightbird." Steele read poetry over spacey music and offered esoteric thoughts between songs. In an adolescent attempt at maturity, as a suburban teenager I had listened to Steele's show, even as it felt beyond my youthful grasp.

But on the December night in question, Steele's normally assured and dreamy voice was shaken as she haltingly informed her listeners that John Lennon had just been shot dead outside the Dakota on Seventy-Second Street. The details were conflicting, but the fact was undeniable.

(Everything that evening happened exactly as I have written above—except that it didn't. Throughout the writing of this book, it has been my habit to quickly fact-check certain easily verifiable details, as I did in this instance. It turns out that Alison Steele was not on the radio that night; in fact, she had ceased to be a DJ entirely the year before. A few minutes' scan on YouTube brought me to the audio recording of a satin-voiced DJ named Vin Scelsa, who had been the one to announce the news of Lennon's assassination on WNEW. That I would have sworn on my children's lives that it had been the Nightbird who relayed the tragic events does nothing to change that it was, in point of fact, not the case. Memory plays tricks. With apologies for the unreliable narration, I return to the story line.)

The Beatles had not occupied any deep place in my life, but Lennon had represented so much hope to a generation and beyond. As the new decade was beginning, something abruptly came to an end. I knew instantly that something profound had changed, something that could not be undone, and it needed to be acknowledged.

The travel writer and novelist Paul Theroux has written about the "lucidity of loneliness" and how it is indispensable in order to experience certain things deeply. I sat on the edge of my bed off Washington Square, enveloped in an eerie sense of aloneness. I often wondered what my classmates in the dorms were doing at any given moment, and I imagined them running out into the hall now and sharing the news, hugs, and tears.

Several days after Lennon's murder, fifty thousand people gathered in Central Park for a ten-minute silent tribute. I didn't go uptown to participate, but I happened to be walking across Washington Square Park at the appointed hour. Without prompting, hundreds of people began to congregate, silently drawn together. I forgot where I was going and stood among others encircling the fountain whose water pipes had been shut off and drained for the winter. Someone played ethereal music softly from a boom box. Otherwise the park stood in silence. I can't say that I prayed, but I've never forgotten standing in solidarity with a group of strangers that afforded me both the relief of anonymity and the intimacy of connection. And like many, I've never been able to walk past the Dakota without thinking of what happened on the sidewalk that night.

As I was finding my footing in New York and at school, my father was losing his way. His business, always a mysterious series of meetings and urgent phone calls, had long resided on a precarious ledge that was beginning to crumble from under him. The official line was that my father "structured tax shelters." I never learned exactly what that meant. What was clear was that my father tried to get money from people for what he called "ventures" and he would take a percentage.

Growing up, few things could elicit more terror in our

home than the sound of the kitchen phone ringing in the evening. "I'M NOT HOME!" would come my father's scream from the bowels of the house. One evening I held the receiver away from my ear as a man unknown to me threatened over the line, "You tell that son of a bitch to call me the minute he gets in."

It's easy to understand how my father gravitated to this line of work, as he was a natural charmer, was always selling, and thought of little other than the big score. There were a few years in my early teens when things seemed to be going his way and we moved from the standard suburban three-bedroom, center-hall Colonial house we had lived in since my birth, located in the perfectly normal town of Westfield, to a long and large house in the horse country of Bernardsville, forty minutes away. (No one in our family rode a horse.)

But without my being aware, things had begun to slip away even before I moved out. That my father had been ruled by his own terrors and insecurities was something I became conscious of only with hindsight.

The first hint of trouble I noticed was when my father began to arrive, unannounced, at my apartment door. Growing up, we rarely spent any time together one-on-one unless we were doing errands or he was driving me to a friend's house. These drop-in visits were always awkward. My inclination was to think it was about me—was I in trouble? Was he checking up on me? He always came to visit on impulse and always without warning; the buzzer simply rang out. Sometimes he said that he had been in the city for a meeting, but other times it was obvious that he had driven in specifically to see me. He never stayed long and usually didn't ask a great deal about what was going on in my life. He always seemed preoccupied. This began to become evident to me the Saturday morning my door buzzed very early.

I had spent the previous night out with Eddie. We had had more to drink than usual and ended up back at my apartment with a six-pack once the bars closed. One wall of my small living room was covered from floor to ceiling with a mirror above and surrounding a wooden mantel that framed a plugged-up fireplace. The mirror had been installed, I presume, to give the cramped room a more spacious feel. My only furnishings were two small faux leather chairs that sat facing the mantel, as if inviting us to enjoy a fire that could never be lit. And there we sat, beer in hand. Until Eddie, unmotivated, reared back and threw his can at the mirror. It was a perfect center shot, directly above the mantel, and the glass shattered into a symmetrical spiderweb from one corner to the other. Eddie was not normally an aggressive person, and I was shocked by his impulsive action. But we were drunk; we shrugged and quickly moved on to other matters.

Now, as I staggered from my bed, hungover, to answer the door, I noticed two things: it was 8:30 in the morning—I had fallen into bed only a few hours earlier—and the mirror covering my wall was shattered. How would I explain this to my father, who was—for a little while longer, at least—paying half my rent?

My father entered and sat in the same chair Eddie had occupied just a short while earlier. He leaned forward, elbows on his knees, staring directly at the splintered mirror and he began to pick his nails—a terrible habit I've inherited. I waited. I studied his fractured reflection from different angles in the shattered glass. His brow furrowed, he seemed distressed. I readied myself for his question about the mirror and the scolding I knew would follow.

But he just chatted for a few minutes about inconsequential things, then stood up and said he had to get back to "your mother," as he always called my mom, and was gone. He never noticed either the destroyed mirror or my shattered state.

The surprise visits continued. One afternoon he was waiting for me in his car outside school. What made this particularly odd was that not only had NYU farmed us out to Circle in the Square, but Circle—because of limited space and more students than it could handle—had also relocated some of our classes to various run-down buildings around Midtown. I was surprised (but probably should not have been) that my father had been able to locate me. Although I remember this visit for another reason. Exiting the building with a female classmate, I heard my father call out his usual greeting: "HEY, PAL!"

Horrified, I said a quick good-bye to my friend and hurried over to silence him.

"She's a cutie," my father said as I arrived curbside.

"Shut up, Dad," I spat at him. "What are you doing here?"

Because my father's opinion still retained, if not direct influence, then at least a lingering emotional resonance in my life, I registered his approval of my attractive classmate—who, it turned out, was Carol, the same young woman who had been kind to me after my run-in with Nikos. Watching her walk away down the street, I felt a sense of protectiveness for Carol and it was in that instant that I realized I had feelings for her.

Carol was slow to reciprocate. We shared all of our acting classes, and in one we worked on a scene together. The play was *Desire under the Elms*, Eugene O'Neill's potboiler with Freudian underpinnings. We were each tasked with a basic acting exercise of following one "objective" to its complete realization. In this case, her character wanted to seduce mine. (I had chosen the scene.) My goal was to resist those advances. Carol would utter such lines as "Oh, Eben, I'm aching for the want of ye" and then lunge for me. My own personal "objective" was in direct odds with that of my character, and invariably Carol and I ended up rolling on the ground, making out in the empty and darkened rehearsal hall.

"You didn't even try to stop me!" Carol, in her innocence, scolded me after each successive rehearsal. I could only shrug and offer to run through it again.

We would go on to date for extended periods over much of the next two decades before we reunited, married, and had a son together. During all of it, Carol played the role of an angel toward me, always protective, caring, and supportive, even when my own behavior was more selfish than loving.

In the spring of that first year in New York, a classmate—a well-muscled, handsome young man named John Robinson—got free tickets to a play at Lincoln Center and invited me along. This was not uncommon, as everyone I knew in school went to the theater as often as they could. But freebies to a Broadway show were a coup.

Until I moved to New York, I had never met anyone who was openly gay. John was, and boasted of the promiscuous sex life he had adopted since coming to the city from Florida. He frequented the gay bars of the West Village and the baths over on St. Mark's Place and was particularly fond of some of the rougher-trade establishments in the dark and mysterious Meat-packing District. John and I weren't close, but we shared acting classes and I enjoyed his company. He knew I had my eye on a couple of the girls in class, and he also knew I was getting nowhere in that regard. I had not considered an alternative to the up-to-now very limited, heterosexual world I inhabited. My first time walking down Christopher Street, passing the Erotic Bakery with its frosted penis and breast cakes in the window, or seeing two men strutting down the street holding hands, clad in Western-style leather chaps—and nothing else—was a startling experience. John occasionally teased me, suggesting that perhaps I was curious about things in his world.

When I agreed to go to the theater, there was no considera-tion that we were on a date, at least not in my mind. We went to the show and then came back downtown. John asked if I had ever been to a gay bar. When I told him that I had not, he suggested we just take in the scene. We went to the Ninth Circle on West Tenth Street. A long bar lined one wall of the narrow room. Everything was painted black; smoke filled the air. The floor was packed tight with men. There was a feeling of restless aggression to the place, but there was an edge to many of the dives that Eddie and I frequented as well. John mentioned there was a back room, then suggested we stay away from it. After a drink, we barhopped down the street to Julius', which seemed not unlike a men's-only version of the Corner Bistro, wooden and warm. It was a pleasant place, but even if this had been something I was interested in, the idea of picking up someone in a bar, a stranger—man or woman—was at this point far beyond anything I could conceive of.

I thanked John for the night out and went to leave. He

shrugged and said, "Can't blame me for trying." We laughed and continued to be friendly. Early in our sophomore year, John got sick and had to take a leave of absence. While he was gone, we learned that his illness had grown more serious and he had returned to his family in Florida. John died.

We didn't yet have a name for what killed him.

The new decade had begun to assert and define itself. In some small ways, so had I. From the comments I received, most of my teachers perceived me to be half-present, if they considered me at all. Yet Terry continued to champion me, and that was all I needed to hold fast to my fledgling belief that this life might be for me. And while other, seemingly more talented and overtly driven students occasionally spoke in hushed voices about perhaps doing or studying something other than acting, I never entertained the notion.

There were occasional moments when it was made clear to me just how focused I was in my own particular way—and how little got through the bubble of my own experience. On the last Monday of March in that first year, walking up Ninth Avenue through Hell's Kitchen, I was on my way to an acting technique class. Belting out the Rolling Stones' recent single, "She's So Cold," I flung open the door to the lobby at Network Studios. The security guard's chair was pulled up close in front of a small television. Many of my classmates were huddled over his shoulder, staring at the screen in disbelief. I stopped singing. "Ronald Reagan has been shot," someone whispered. The event seemed so remote, so removed from the reality I existed in, that the intensity of the others' reactions shocked me. I simply could not understand their concern or what it had to do with our life.

One afternoon, not long after the assassination attempt on Reagan, I was looking out my fourth-story window when I recognized the slouching saunter of my former theater history teacher, Mel Gordon, who was walking down on the street below. I opened the window and shouted down to him. I doubt he recognized me at such a distance—if he ever knew me at all—but he stopped when he heard his name. Leaning out the window, I called down to him again. Now he looked up. Like a lunatic, I leaned out even farther and waved my greeting. Gazing up, he shielded his eyes from the sun and called back, without missing a beat, "What a place to die!" and resumed his ambling. I laughed and ducked back inside. I didn't die in that apartment. On the contrary: like the '80s, I was just waking up.

A day at the beach, 1981.

Sparking It

I HADN'T GROWN up in a movie-loving household. Save for *Casablanca*, I can't recall my father ever encouraging me to sit and watch a film with him. Other than her playful crushes on Robert Redford and Steve McQueen—crushes my father didn't accept in a similarly playful vein—my mother never mentioned any movies. We didn't talk about current hits at the dinner table, and I don't remember my parents ever going out to the cinema. So it was a revelation to discover the world of old Hollywood when Eddie first brought me to Theatre 80 on St. Mark's Place in the East Village to see a *Thin Man* double feature with William Powell and Myrna Loy. While I was eager to attend my Monday, Wednesday, and Friday acting classes, my academic commitments the other two days of the week were of little interest. Instead, I became a disciple of the Tuesday and Thursday afternoon double bill when I was meant to be in English or history class. *On the Waterfront* coupled with *A Streetcar Named Desire*, *East of Eden* and *Rebel without a Cause*, *All about Eve* and

Sunset Boulevard, The Maltese Falcon after *Treasure of the Sierra Madre*. At Circle in the Square I was learning how to act. But it was at the revival houses that I learned what a movie star was: how they held the screen, pulling everyone toward them. Emerging back out into the sunlight after hours in the dark, I felt privately powerful. I wandered the streets in a reverie of possibility.

I don't tend to be a nostalgic person—I spend little time pining for things from "back in the day" or lamenting the changing of the guard—but the disappearance of the revival movie house, once a staple of New York City, is a loss. Planning my day—my week—around a particular showtime filled the event with import that was difficult to ignore. Easily some of my happiest and most expansive moments were spent in the dark. Sometimes it was up at the Hollywood Twin on Eighth Avenue and Forty-Seventh Street or way uptown at the Thalia, but usually I was at the 8th Street Playhouse, occasionally with a friend but more often alone. I went there to meet with Marlon Brando, James Dean, Katharine Hepburn, and James Stewart. Deeper probing rewarded me with cinematic riches. I discovered the silent genius of Buster Keaton and Harold Lloyd. Like so many before me, the magic of the dark room, with those flickering black-and-white images, revealed a world I could escape into but also, especially when alone, one I secretly imagined myself inhabiting with a pure and unapologetic joy. I scarcely dared to picture myself as towering as those I worshipped on the screen, but when alone in the dark that distance between us seemed to recede, my pure appreciation and wonder bridging any gap, at least for a few hours.

I also became a regular at the second act of nearly every show on Broadway. Early on, a classmate had complained how expensive theater tickets were, to which my teacher Terry Hayden simply said, "The second act is free."

"What do you mean?" I asked.

"Go up at intermission, wait around, and when the lights go down, grab a seat." I hung on most things Terry said, and this one she didn't have to say twice.

No one else from class was interested in potentially getting arrested, or at the very least being hissed at by an irate theater manager. But my friend Mickey, with whom I smoked pot and threw Frisbee in the park, was always up for a thrill—if not necessarily the theater itself—and joined me on occasion. Just as often I went on my own.

I'd simply call the theater where the show I was interested in was being performed, ask when intermission was, ride the subway uptown, and wait in the shadows across the street. At the appointed time, the theater doors swung open. Patrons stepped out to get some air or grab a smoke. I crossed over and mingled with the crowd, heart beating. When the lights blinked off to indicate the imminent start of the second act, I filed back in with the crowd. To justify my loitering in the back, I often made a show of looking impatiently around for a nonexistent companion to return from the bathroom. When the lights began to dim, I slipped into the closest open seat. The curtain went up. Easy.

I saw half of Elizabeth Taylor's performance in *The Little Foxes*; she was difficult to hear and stunning to watch. I sat as close to the stage as possible for Al Pacino, thrilled when spittle landed on me in the front row as he explosively cursed,

"Fucking Ruthie!" in *American Buffalo*. David Bowie's elegant and sinewy physicality as *The Elephant Man* has remained with me. I experienced Lauren Bacall hold the theater in her hand, and watched Katharine Hepburn give the most humble curtain call I ever saw when she stood, without bowing, and whispered, "Thanks," to an adoring audience. I saw Lena Horne sing half her show and bare her heart. I saw the second halves of both hits and bombs.

On several occasions I attended the second act of a play called *Agnes of God*, costarring a young actress named Amanda Plummer. Amanda won a Tony Award for her role as a disturbed nun, and I was captivated by her performance. One evening after the show, I waited by the stage door at the Music Box Theatre. A petite young woman appeared and, after signing a few autographs, quickly scurried down Forty-Fifth Street. I caught up to her and told her how much I enjoyed her work. She thanked me and kept moving.

It had taken me a moment to recognize her, because in what seemed like some kind of extraordinary magic trick, Amanda had appeared so much larger onstage, almost to the point of being huge.

As a child I had experienced a similar moment of shape-shifting alchemy myself. One night I lay on my front lawn in midwinter, the ground covered with a hard layer of snow. On my back, limbs outstretched, I was trying to make snow angels. I didn't weigh enough to break through the thin crust of ice, so I quit trying. I lay still and stared up into the clear night sky. It was perhaps the first time I had really taken in the stars, and as I gazed longer, I began to experience what felt like a morphing of my physical size. I seemed to swell and grow and become massive, then recede back, only to swell up again. I rode the sensation like a wave for what felt like a long time. Staring up at the stars flickering light-years away, I understood myself to be deeply and powerfully alone. Yet in the same instant I was aware of something beyond my normal grasp, something in me connecting to a sensation of safety and a joy I could not understand, but was wise enough in my youth not to need an explanation. Until adolescence, I experienced similar moments of seeming shape-shifting and felt an accessibility to something powerful. Perhaps what I had experienced was what the Gnostic Christians of the second century called the "spark of the divine." And I wonder if the very best of acting doesn't contain a bit of that spark.

Whatever it was, I wanted to be near it.

Still following Amanda, I blurted out, "Would you like to have a cup of coffee?"

Amanda stopped and turned to me. Smiling shyly she said, "No, thank you. I have to go." She was gracious and then gone.

I spent the summer after that first year of school waiting tables out on Long Island, in Southampton. My parents had moved there as full-time residents, which, in the intricate social structure of the Hamptons, was a very different thing from the folks who descended on Memorial Day Weekend, vanished on Labor Day, and looked down on the year-rounders. My parents had moved into an old, rambling house. My bedroom had doors on both ends, and you could pass through to get from the front of the house to the back. Soon after my arrival, sensing that the tension and strain emanating from my father had vastly increased during the year of my absence, I sat on the edge of my bed and swung open both doors.

"I've got to keep the doors open in this house," I said aloud to myself, aware that my literal action was referring to a metaphorical desire. My noble but misguided intention was quickly dashed when I fell in with a drinking and pot-smoking crowd from the restaurant; soon my bedroom doors were closed and locked and I couldn't wait to get back to the city.

As my second year of school began, my friend Eddie headed off on a trip around the world. (He would make it as far as his first stop, Bangkok, and stay there for two years.) Before leaving, he sublet me the bedroom of his fifth-floor walk-up in the West Village, on the corner of Bank and West Fourth Streets. My room had an unobstructed view of the Empire State Building, and I would lie in bed and watch its lights go out at midnight. Whereas my first apartment had always felt temporary, on Bank Street I felt I had landed. New York was my home. The only hiccup was that Eddie had neglected to inform his roommate, who was out of the city working for a time, that a schoolkid would be living in the other bedroom upon his return.

Tommy was nearly a decade older than I was. Like Eddie, he was from Dallas. Unlike Eddie, he had no interest in associating with me. Tommy was just coming off work as an assistant editor on *Ragtime*, a big feature film. He saw his life going in a direction that did not include living with a teenager.

Tommy was tightly wound and not known for his stoicism. Our small living room was taken up in large part by his drum kit. More than once the beat woke me in the middle of the night as Tommy pounded out his frustrations, which seemed plentiful. No one ever called the police on us for his midnight jam sessions. Greenwich Village would remain a quirky, strangely tolerant neighborhood for a little while longer.

As my classes resumed, one in particular got my attention. It was curated more than taught by a playwright named Albert Innaurato. Albert was a large man with a bizarre sense of humor and a unique view on reality. He was given to wild insecurities and self-loathing, which he wore on his sleeve. Apropos of nothing, Albert often proclaimed, "Soon death, then nothing." He loved the opera, his neurosis, and young men. He'd recently had a hit on Broadway with a play called *Gemini*. One day he invited one of its stars to come in to speak to the class.

Reed Birney was just several years older than us. He seemed normal enough, and told us that the distance between where he was and where we were was not so great. He was the first embodiment of the professional success I wanted that seemed close enough to relate to. I remember thinking, "Maybe..."

Three decades after our first and only encounter, we met again when I directed Reed in a television show. I shared with him the effect his visit had on me as a young student. By then Reed had survived a career as a journeyman actor only to win a Tony Award and become a success "overnight." (Soon after our reunion, Reed starred on Broadway in a play in which my daughter also appeared. I got to see Reed's performance a dozen times and can confirm what a rich actor he has grown into—to say nothing of life coming full circle.)

Albert Innaurato was to play a still larger role in my life than merely exposing me to Reed. In the late spring of my sophomore year he phoned me out of the blue. He had a new play being presented at Playwrights Horizons, one of New York's premier off-Broadway theaters. It was (poorly) titled *Herself as Lust*, about a female sculptor who takes in a runaway kid with whom she begins an affair. The actor playing the teenage lead was pushing thirty. As the play was nearing the end of its modestly successful run, Albert was curious if a real teenager might evoke a more emotional reaction to his play. Would I be interested in appearing in the final two performances? I would need to learn the entire play and blocking in less than a week, would have one rehearsal on the stage with the lead actress, the other actors I would be meeting for the first time in front of an audience. Naturally, I leapt at the opportunity.

I holed up in a small rehearsal space at NYU and corralled my friend and classmate Billy Tucker to run the lines and staging with me for hours each day. Billy was an army brat, leading-man handsome, reserved, and as close a friend as I had at school.

The lead actress in the play (understandably) had little interest in breaking in a new cast member on the final weekend of performances, but marked me through the paces once. I had continued to study with Terry Hayden and at the last minute invited her to see the show. She was unavailable. I went on in a blur. I remember little except sweating profusely because I forgot to take off the heavy winter sweater I had been given to make my initial entrance in. After my second performance Terry was waiting in the lobby to congratulate me. That she had changed her plans and deemed me worthy of her time validated me beyond her supportive words. Her presence made what had happened somehow real, gave it resonance, and empowered me when I walked across the street to meet with the playwright for a drink after the show.

At the West Bank Cafe, Albert praised my work as well as himself for casting me despite complaints from those around him about hiring an untested boy. He had future hopes for the play, he explained, and I expressed my interest to be involved. Later my friend Billy, who had joined us for a drink, told me how surprised he was by the way I spoke to Albert in the bar.

"What do you mean?" I asked.

"I had no idea you were so ambitious. I mean, you were really direct with him."

Billy and I had been classmates for nearly two years at this point, and we had been roommates on Washington Place for a semester. He knew me as well as anyone at school knew me. His shock at my aspirations speaks to the disconnect that still existed between the life that was bubbling inside me and the one I presented to the world.

Not long after my successful turn in Albert's show, Playwrights Horizons invited me to audition for another one of their productions. I didn't get the part, but some weeks later I received a plain white postcard in the mail. It was from the casting director at the theater, a man named John Lyons. On it, beneath the typed, boilerplate "Thank you for auditioning" formality, he had handwritten a note to me: "Although this didn't happen, I want you to know that you are a talented young actor and should pursue a career in the theatre…"

During this second year of school, I also had my first close encounter with Hollywood stardom. It jogged right past me on three different occasions. Five flights below me, in the vegetarian restaurant across the street from my apartment on the corner of Bank and West Fourth Streets, on a warm autumn night, Al Pacino was filming a scene from his upcoming movie, *Author! Author!* At this point in time, there was no actor alive on the planet more important to me than Al Pacino. I went down to watch. With a few dozen others, I saw my hero jog past on the way from his trailer to the restaurant for filming. A short while later, when there was a pause in the proceedings, the same action was repeated in reverse as he jogged back past

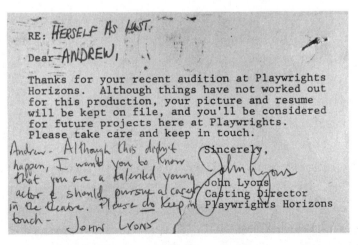

The most inspiring rejection I ever got.

us to his trailer while they moved the cameras or whatever it was they did between shots.

Playing Pacino's son in the scene was a young actor around my age named Eric Gurry. Between setups, Eric loitered out in the street. During one break I summoned courage and walked over to him. I, too, was an actor, I told him, studying at NYU. It was evident that Eric was not interested in our chat, but in an effort to bridge the void between where he stood and I hovered, I stuck out my hand. He stopped and looked at it and then into my eyes. He seemed to consider something and then took my proffered hand. Eric was called back to work and I shuffled back to the other side of the street and waited for Pacino to trot past, which he did a few more times—until I was the last fool standing on the street, watching through the restaurant window as night gave way and filming finally wrapped up.

It was my first exposure to a film set, and while I was—in every sense—on the outside looking in, everything about it was of interest to me. As it is to this day.

The next morning in school, I got up in front of my voice class like a kid doing show-and-tell and described my night in all its detail. Passion and excitement heightened what might have otherwise come across as a childish account. My enthusiasm was contagious and the room was electric in my retelling. I had made my first contact, and it was thrilling.

Not long after this I was attending a wedding, and luck or fate seated me next to an agent at a small commercial agency. She gave me her number. I called. Soon she had procured an audition for me for an industrial film. Industrial films were used for training purposes, marketing, education. They were usually fairly dry, short, and not for public broadcast. I have no recollection of what the film was about, but I cannot forget my one line.

The scene centered around a kitchen table. It was breakfast time. My character was eating cereal, and the woman playing my mother was busy at the kitchen sink when she casually asked me, "Did you fill the car with gas last night, like your father asked you to?"

My response, and the entirety of my part: "... He *did*?"

My first and only instinct—and here I unwittingly employed lessons from my early training by drawing from personal experience with my own father—was to deliver the line with absolute terror. I swallowed hard and whispered the two words. I got the job. And I write this next phrase without arrogance: I knew I would.

It was the first of so many times when I simply knew when a part was mine. There would be instances when I would be more prepared, more set up for success, more desired for a role, perform better, yet not get the part. And there have been times when it seems the air has been cleared and things come as if ordained. I have never been able to explain it. Sometimes a part simply has your name on it—or it doesn't.

The day of the shoot, I was excited but held myself in check, watching. We rehearsed the scene; I was seated with my back to the window. Then someone with a walkie-talkie sent me away to be made ready. It was the first time anyone other than my mother or myself had combed my hair. The camera rolled and I delivered my one line. They adjusted something with the camera and we did another take and I did it again, then again. The director then said to me, "Okay, I've got that, now give me another reading."

I had no idea what he meant. I had interpreted the part and the line to be done this way. I had no alternatives. After several more takes in which I performed the line with the exact same quiet, guilty dread, the director wisely declared success and moved on.

What I got out of the deal was close to a hundred dollars, my first experience in front of the camera, and my contract, which I could take to the Screen Actors Guild to prove that I had completed a professional job on film and was now eligible to join the professional actors union.

Union membership cost more than my salary. I tried to convince my father to loan me the rest of the money. But as an actor is allowed one job without joining the union, my father insisted I wait to pay until I got a second job, which struck him as unlikely. My justification for joining now was simple: all professional actors are in the union. If I didn't consider myself a professional, why should anyone else? I needed to be in the union. My mother quietly gave me the money. I was now a pro.

My roommate Tommy and I had begun to find some common ground, and one day he asked me if I wanted to join him for a screening he had been invited to attend. I had never been to a private screening of a movie. As we entered a Midtown office tower, I was confused: How could there be a movie theater in an office building? Up on the fourteenth floor, a door led to a fairly long room with a few dozen very comfortable-looking chairs and a screen at the far end. There was no popcorn machine in sight.

Two skinny young guys got up to address the ten or fifteen people in attendance. Finishing each other's sentences, they thanked everyone for coming and described their efforts to make a new kind of film. What we were about to see was the result of a few days' shooting.

Apparently I was at a fund-raising event. The lights went down and the brief promo reel began. The images on-screen were eerie, tense: a very close shot of a car tire racing down a yellow line at night; the head of a shovel scraping along pavement, its sound high-pitched and harsh; the camera tracking with it low to the ground. A door in the dark; shots rang out and holes appeared, casting smoky beams of light. Shot after tense shot, unlike anything I had seen before. Clearly these two skinny guys had a singular point of view.

"I'd go see it," I said to Tommy as the lights went up.

The two skinny guys were the Coen brothers, Joel and Ethan, and the film they were trying to raise money for was their first, *Blood Simple*. Taking questions, a guest asked if something in a particular shot was done on purpose. As Ethan shook his head, Joel looked at him and said, "There were no accidents."

These two were not that much older than me, yet they were taking themselves very seriously in their work and were confident in their abilities to carry it out. I was far too shy or intimidated to meet them that day (and I never have), as they appeared to reside on a distant shore, across an ocean of uncertainty.

Early on in this second year of school, something happened that, while beneficial, would later serve as a catalyst for a destructive pattern I was stuck in for some time. Although a fairly consistent pot smoker since my middle teens, now whenever I smoked I would get paranoid and sink into deep pits of loneliness. In a lucid moment a radical thought occurred to me: I should stop smoking pot. My brilliant strategy proved effective. I stopped getting paranoid, and even though I spent a great deal of time alone, I ceased to feel lonely.

I would later use this recollection of easy and painless withdrawal from marijuana as justification during several crucial years once my drinking took off. "I just put down pot when it stopped being fun," I would tell myself. "I'll do the same with drinking." But a decade later those feelings of loneliness I just boasted of rarely experiencing would return in the form of deep isolation and despair. That loneliness was induced by alcohol, which would prove a much more cunning foe than those loose joints I had bought in the park.

By now I had drifted fully into my own life, and the thought of returning to my parents' house between school sessions simply never occurred to me. Years later my younger brother, Justin, said, "Peter and Stephen came back every summer during school. I always expected you'd do the same, but you were just gone."

Discovering myself in the world and developing my own

way of navigating through it, my sights were set completely forward. However, my school status seemed in some question. I had been placed on academic probation on my arrival two years earlier and had never earned my way off it. It was a problem.

Then I got a call.

SAG & OPEN, "CLASS"

8/10 from 10 AM-2 PM (SAG) and 2-6 PM (open) at Guild Studios, Ansonia Hotel, 73 St. & B'way.
A SAG & open call for the feature film, "Class," will be held on Tues. Aug. 10 at Guild Studios, Ansonia Hotel, Broadway & 73 St.: SAG actors will be seen from 10 AM-2 PM; non-SAG actors will be seen from 2-6 PM. Character breakdown—**Jonathon:** 18-year-old prep school student, extremely intelligent, but insecure when it comes to peer pressure and dating; **Skip:** Jonathon's 18-year-old roommate and best friend, upper-class, old-money wealth, attractive and charming. Only actors who are 25 years-old or younger will be seen.

This little ad changed everything forever.

My friend Billy, who had helped me prepare for Albert's play, wanted to tell me about an ad he'd seen in *Backstage* for a movie that was casting. *Backstage* was a weekly newspaper that catered to people aspiring to be in show business. It featured interviews with moderately—and sometimes more than moderately—successful actors, and there were advertisements for acting, singing, and dancing classes. There was also a section on casting calls open to the public.

"They're looking for someone eighteen, vulnerable, and sensitive to be in this movie," Billy told me.

I would go if he would, I said. But besides looking twenty-five, Billy was also not in SAG, and it was a union audition. Since I was a SAG member, thanks to my two-word performance in the industrial film, I qualified. The "open call" was being held at the Ansonia hotel up on Seventy-Third Street—the same building where the summer acting program I attended a few years earlier had been located. I took the number 1 train uptown, retraced my steps through Needle Park, and entered the Beaux Arts building.

Hundreds of other eighteen-year-old, vulnerable, and sensitive-looking kids were leaning, sitting, slouching along the walls of the narrow corridor, waiting their turns. I turned around and left.

Back out on the street, I stopped. I was an idiot: Did I think there would be no one there?

Throughout this time, people appeared to offer assistance or point the way just enough for me to move to the next signpost. But standing on the street corner now, I was on my own. Standing across the street from where I had been hustled out of all my cash in the three-card monte game a few years earlier, I looked down at the brand-new 8x10 black-and-white head shot I'd recently had taken. An actor wasn't an actor without an 8x10, and Billy and a few other classmates had recently had their photos done and encouraged me to do the same. My glossy gaze stared directly back at me, clear-eyed and open, slightly overwhelmed, a little scared around the mouth, but very present.

I walked back in, flopped down on the dirty carpet at the end of the line, and waited. Nobody spent more than a few minutes inside the room at the end of the hall. When my turn finally came, I sat across a folding table from a man with wavy hair. The man, whose name I would later learn was David Rubin, asked where I was from.

I answered.

He asked where I went to school.

I answered.

Having exhausted our conversation, he asked if that was my head shot I was clutching in my hand. Yes, I said. I uncrumpled my photo with a brand-new, freshly typed résumé attached to the back, smoothed it out, and handed it over.

There was one thing on my résumé: Albert's play. The rest of the page was blank. After only two performances, it was a bit confident to claim it—but, hell, who would ever know?

"You spelled the author's name wrong," David said.

"What?"

" 'Innaurato' has two *n*'s."

Oh.

There seemed nothing more to say and I got up to leave.

"Hold on," David said. He turned over his shoulder to a woman with a wild head of hair who was sitting behind him. She was facing away from us, on the phone. He tapped her shoulder and she glanced at him. He nodded my way. Her eyes met mine for an instant before I looked away. I could feel her give David a distracted nod and return her attention to the phone.

"Can you come to our office on Monday?" David asked.

"Um, sure," I mumbled.

"Do you have a pen? Write down the address."

I didn't have one.

"Here, I'll write it." His tone was gentle, as if he were

ANDREW McCARTHY

My first head shot.

talking to a skittish dog. He took a scrap and wrote an address on Fifty-Seventh Street and told me to be there at 2:00 p.m.

I have no recollection of my feet touching the ground until I got back downtown.

By 1:00 p.m. on Monday, I was waiting outside the building on Fifty-Seventh Street. At exactly two o'clock, I walked through the revolving door and approached the uniformed guard at the reception desk. I told him who I was there to see. He put the receiver to his ear and dialed. We waited. His eyes never left me. I felt my leg shaking under my baggy pants and became convinced it was all a mistake. Those people I had met at the Ansonia did not intend for me to come here; they probably didn't even work here. This was an apartment building, for God's sake. What was I doing? I had misunderstood. I was about to make a fool of myself.

The doorman jerked his chin at me. "What's your name?"

"Uh…"

"Your name."

I told him. He repeated it into the receiver. He listened for a moment, squinting at me. He hung up.

"Thirty-third floor. Apartment E," the guard said.

The door was brown metal. I knocked. David greeted me warmly and invited me in. I was in an apartment that seemed to have been converted into an office. Up two steps on a landing, in front of a wall of windows, were a couple of desks and several large metal racks filled with binders and stacks and stacks of actors' head shots—hundreds of them, just like mine.

The woman with wild hair was there and on the phone again. She hung up and came to shake my hand. Her name was Mary Goldberg.

She gave me two brief scenes that must have been from the movie script and told me to sit in the corner and look them over. After scanning them a few times, I said I was ready.

"Already? You sure?"

"Yup." I was jumping out of my skin. The longer I sat there, the worse it was getting. My thinking at this point was to just get it over with.

I read the scenes with David.

"That was very good," Mary said when I finished. She sounded surprised. She was not half as surprised as I was.

"Okay," I mumbled.

"The director, Lew, is coming to town in a few days. I'd like you to meet him."

"Sounds good." I shrugged. I resisted leaping across the table to hug her.

A few days later, I was standing in the lobby of the Parker Meridien Hotel, farther along Fifty-Seventh Street.

"Bone-jour, Parker Meridien, how may I help you?" said the decidedly nasal New York–accented operator on the other end of the lobby phone. I told her who I was and who I was there to see.

"All right, Andrew. You better go on up, then." She gave me a room number and up I went. I knocked on the door. After a long while, David opened the door.

"Oh, you're here. Uh, can you just wait in the hall for a few minutes?"

Apparently, I was supposed to announce myself from the lobby. I would then be called up when they were ready. I flopped down in yet another hallway and waited. In time, another young man about my age—who I assumed to be an actor meeting for the same role—came out of the room and passed me without acknowledging my existence. After another minute David opened the door and invited me in to meet the director.

It was a large suite. A set of couches flanked a glass coffee table. A few chairs were pulled up close. Mary was seated off to the side, where she could see everything. She greeted me and introduced me to a small man with a closely cropped salt-and-pepper beard. Lewis John Carlino rose from one of the couches to greet me. He was soft-spoken, with a gentle demeanor. Lewis had written and directed a brilliant movie called *The Great Santini*, with Robert Duvall, and directed another very '70s film called *The Sailor Who Fell from Grace with the Sea*, starring Kris Kristofferson.

I sat on the other couch. We chatted. Lewis described something about the plot of the movie and I nodded along, not registering a word he said.

As I was leaving, Mary suggested I come in the next day and be put on videotape. It was a new audition tool and they could take the tape back to Los Angeles and view it with the producers. I would be doing the same two scenes I had done in Mary's office. I was not offered a script. I promised I'd be at the place David wrote down for me, and at the appointed time.

When I was a young actor, I had an unconscious habit, born of tension, of making my eyes go very wide into a glazed stare. I first became aware of this the following day in a small, all-white room as I stood just a few feet in front of a bulky video camera and read the two scenes with stilted formality.

"Just relax your eyes and try again," Lewis said.

I nodded my understanding at his direction but had no idea what he was talking about.

Whereas up to now everything had passed in an exciting blur of disorienting abstraction, suddenly it was all too real.

Gone was any sense of fluid, innocent glee over my unlikely circumstances—I was just an amateur student actor in over his head. Lewis was polite. Mary was discouraged. David looked away. Gone was their "I wonder if maybe…" excitement from my earlier meetings. I was dismissed. It was over.

For several weeks I wallowed in a funk of despair. It had been an impossible long shot, yet somewhere it had felt so right, so like what was supposed to become of me. Underneath my dejection seeped a growing dread that I didn't have what it would take to carry me toward the only thing I had found that made me feel like *me*. If I couldn't have that, what was to become of me? What was I even doing studying acting?

That question, at least, seemed to be answering itself. Apparently I would not be studying acting. The failure to improve my academic standing was not going to be ignored any longer. NYU would attempt to struggle on without me.

It was a hot late-summer day, and I was sweating as I climbed the five flights to Tommy's apartment. (It was always Tommy's apartment.) I pushed the door open—we never locked it—and went to the kitchen for some water. Tommy was slumped in his usual spot by the window, staring out. He ignored my entrance, as he usually did. Tommy had been unemployed for some time and his mood was often dark as he waited for the phone to ring.

Tommy was the first person I knew who owned a telephone answering machine. Located on the floor just inside his bedroom, it sat in a tangle of cords. Early on in our cohabitation, I forgot to give him a message regarding possible work; consequently he forbade me any further use of said machine.

Reciprocally, he usually neglected to mention if someone had left a message for me. This was not out of any spite but simply because it was understood between us that his life was more important than mine. However, recently my mother had complained that I hadn't returned her calls (a pattern that has not improved with the years). When I gingerly mentioned this to Tommy, he promised to make more of an effort with my messages.

I stood over the kitchen sink swilling water, wondering how I would fill the rest of my afternoon...week...life, when Tommy spoke for the first time since my arrival.

"Oh, you got a call on the machine," he murmured from under his cloud.

"Really? Who?"

"About some audition or something."

The glass stopped halfway to my mouth. There had only been one audition. I walked cautiously out of the kitchen and looked at my roommate. He jerked his chin toward the machine. I stepped to his room, crouched down, and hit the rewind button. I scrolled back through a message, then another. Then another. Each a message for my roommate.

"When was it?"

"I don't know. Yesterday? Maybe a few days ago." Tommy had returned to his own dark internal reverie.

My natural rhythm up to that point had been a series of meandering, accidental-seeming advances achieved at the last possible instant, and then unfocused episodes with things sliding away. What I was to experience now was a big bang that exploded with a force that has sustained all that has followed.

David Rubin's voice was on Tommy's machine, suggesting that I might remember him from a movie audition a month or six weeks earlier. He was wondering if I could give him a call back if I got the chance.

I called. It was a wrong number.

I ran for a pen and listened to the message again. I wrote the number on my palm.

David was glad I had called. They had no idea how to find me and had just about given up hope. Would I mind coming in again?

Apparently, back in Los Angeles, when the entire creative team was viewing auditions, mine came up and the director suggested they skip it. But in these early days of the VCR, no one in the room knew how to fast-forward the tape. They were forced to watch my audition again to get to the next one.

The producer, Marty Ransohoff, had not been in New York. We had never met. But he was in that room in Los Angeles and saw the tape. Marty—a large man with a terrible comb-over and a brusque manner—was old-school Hollywood. He had made himself rich producing television shows like *The Beverly Hillbillies* and *Mister Ed*, the talking horse show. He also had aspirations and produced such early antiwar films as *The Americanization of Emily* and *Catch-22*. "Who's that kid with the crazy eyes?" Marty apparently said upon seeing my audition. "Kid's weird. Those crazy eyes remind me of a young Tony Perkins."

No one else, before or after, has ever compared me to Anthony Perkins.

I auditioned again. Then suddenly I was in Chicago, where

the film was to begin shooting in a few weeks. The movie was called *Class,* and it centered around a young working-class kid who goes off to a posh boarding school. Through a series of very unlikely circumstances, he ends up having an ongoing affair with his roommate's mother.

The casting process had been narrowed down to four actors for the two lead roles. We were broken into pairs. I was teamed with an impossibly handsome young actor named Rob Lowe who was auditioning to play my rich roommate and the son of the woman with whom my character would have an affair.

I was back in the dizzy and disorienting world of "What the hell is going on and how did I get here?"—which suited my character perfectly. Rob and I were sent off to spend an hour together in an effort to create chemistry while the other pair of actors were put through their paces. We wandered through nearby Water Tower Place, where I was soon to shoot a memorable (at least to me) love scene in a glass elevator.

Rob had recently costarred in Francis Ford Coppola's soon-to-be-released movie adaptation of *The Outsiders,* so he held forth from a place of Hollywood experience as we drifted over the polished marble of the mall, killing time. He spoke of Tom and Matt and dinner with Francis. I was unsure exactly whom he was talking about but nodded my head anyway. While a part of me wondered how much of Rob's banter was simply whistling in the dark and how much was a belief in his destiny, another part of me simply envied his apparent ease and confidence. I said little. While a charming bravado may have been Rob's preferred method of making himself ready, mine was to go quiet and become hyper-observant—of those around me as well as myself. I don't believe either one of us thought to actually rehearse the scenes together.

After the audition, I waited in my hotel room for word to come down. In less than an hour, the phone rang.

The part was mine.

I called my parents, but it was difficult for my mother to understand what I was saying, since I was jumping up and down trying to touch the ceiling with my palm for some reason, my energy too much to contain.

I was wildly thrilled, of course, but somewhere inside me I was not surprised. My private ambition, coupled with last-second, almost ordained assistance from others—coupled with remote feelings of certainty and connection to something beyond myself—all seemed to coalesce at this instant. My sneaking premonition from a few years earlier that I would attend college for two years and then be a professional actor had just materialized. I had, of course, no idea how this would come to pass, but there had been a naïve belief—an understanding—that could not be dismissed as arrogance or even confidence. I possessed the youthful gift of not yet being aware of what was and was not possible. There is great power in innocence.

But the producers had neglected to mention one last hurdle. I was to be flown to Los Angeles to meet the woman whom *Newsweek* magazine had recently declared "the most beautiful film actress of all time." Jacqueline Bisset, at thirty-eight, was nearly double my age. She had starred in numerous movies, including *Day for Night, Rich and Famous, Bullitt,* as well as *The Deep,* which spawned a thousand wet T-shirt contests. Jacqueline had final approval over who was to play her young lover. I was assured it was just a formality.

"Just relax, kid. Jackie's gonna love you," Marty said to me as we drove in his Jaguar up Benedict Canyon in Beverly Hills. Watching his fingers drum the steering wheel at a red light, it felt like much more than a formality.

The door to Jacqueline Bisset's Spanish bungalow was answered by an Adonis with shoulder-length blond hair. Alexander Godunov was a world-famous ballet star who had recently defected from Russia. He had landed on his feet as Jackie's live-in lover. Alexander escorted Marty and me into the sunken living room and was gone. I perched on the edge of an ottoman. Marty lowered himself into a large chair in the corner. We waited.

"Relax, kid," Marty wisely advised me again.

Alexander returned, silently handed me a glass of water, then vanished again.

"Call me Jackie," the casually elegant British woman said as she strode across the room, hand outstretched.

After she sat down, Jackie squinted her blue eyes at me from the couch and I knew that falling in love with this older woman would require very little acting. I said something innocuous and Jackie turned to Marty. "He's cheeky."

And that was that.

"Nice work, kid," Marty said as we climbed back into his Jaguar.

For my one-night visit to LA, I had been placed at the Chateau Marmont, perhaps Hollywood's most notorious hotel and the site of John Belushi's recent overdose. It was a fifteen-minute drive from Jackie's home in the hills. Whereas Marty had picked me up before the meeting, on the return trip he dropped me off at a taxi stand down the hill from Jackie's place, tossed me a ten-dollar bill, and advised me to grab a cab the rest of the way back to my hotel.

Welcome to Hollywood, kid.

Attempting It

MY FIRST DAY on the set of a feature film was spent in bra and panties. My second day as well. Perhaps the thinking was to begin with complete humiliation so that things could only get better. The scene in question involved a prank played on my character, Jonathan, by Rob Lowe's character, Skip. Skip tells Jonathan that, in accordance with school tradition, everyone must don women's underwear and parade around the Quad on the first day of school. Being utterly naïve and wanting to fit in, Jonathan put on the ladies' undergarments provided by Skip, who then locks him out in the crowded Quad for the entire student body to mock.

It's a common complaint that school doesn't prepare you for the real world, and acting school certainly does not prepare you for filmmaking, but it's doubtful much could have prepared me for running around in front of hundreds of extras in my black, lacy finest. The indignity began in the wardrobe fitting when I was given a G-string to wear under my panties to smooth out any bumps that might prove too graphic. The

First day on set.

wardrobe designer was a lovely and flamboyant gentleman who handled the whole thing with grace and humor while I stood frozen under his inspection. Someone asked how I had slept and I confessed that I hadn't gotten much rest in anticipation of the first day. It was suggested that next time I masturbate—"to take the edge off." I nodded at this insight and tried to breathe. The men in the sound department then inspected my skimpy wardrobe, shook their collective heads, and concluded in dismay that I was going to need the "rectal mic." It took me some time to realize this was a joke.

The next day wasn't much better. In filmmaking there is a fairly set procedure. After rehearsing a scene with the director, the crew is called in to watch, at which point pieces of colored tape are put down on the floor to indicate where each actor moves and stands. These bits of tape are called "marks." In this way the cinematographer knows where to put the camera and focus the lights. Consequently, consistency to an actor's movement is essential. I had no idea about this. If the impulse struck me to go to a different place during a particular "take," I simply did so, thinking I was keeping things fresh and alive; instead, I was walking into unlit corners. When I walked right out of one shot entirely, the gruff and charming cinematographer, Ric Waite, snapped, "Hey! Andy, where the hell are you going?"

Tension is the enemy of good acting, and so much of what needed to happen to achieve the shots seemed designed to create tension and be counterproductive to relaxed and creative acting work. Even the call of "ACTION!" at the start of a scene rattled me.

(One day, when my daughter was visiting the set of a television show I was directing, she asked why I always softly said "…and…" before I quietly said "…action." Only in that instant did it occur to me that I was attempting to soften the moment of beginning to an almost invisible transition between before and during, all in an effort to lessen feelings of tension.)

A sense of privacy—a working belief that you and your acting partner are the only ones in the room—is also conducive to a convincing performance. It is one of the most difficult things to accomplish. Easy enough to understand when you consider there's a large camera that's being manned by several people, a grotesque microphone hanging from a pole extended over your head, a wall of large, blazing lights surrounded by a spiderweb of flags to create natural-looking shadows, all focused on you. It followed that I needed to find a way to reconcile these necessary technical distractions with the work I was tasked with accomplishing. But I just couldn't shake the feeling that the camera was staring at me. I needed help.

During my second year of school, I had begun to attend a Saturday morning acting class with my teacher Terry Hayden and her occasional teaching partner Jacqueline Brookes. Brookes was a working actress, and her pragmatic manner made her an ideal foil for Terry's velvet-fisted touch. It was she who made what may seem an odd suggestion, one that made perfect sense nonetheless.

In the Method school of acting, one of the exercises is the imagined creation of a simple object: the actor sits in a chair and tries to conjure an apple, for example—the weight, feel, and texture, even the taste—through the five senses. If you were to walk into an acting class while this work was going on, you might see a row of students sitting in chairs, their eyes closed, their empty hands held out in front of them, touching something only they could see and feel. Strasberg and then Terry took it further and made that simple object a personal one in order to elicit an emotional reaction. That way, if the actor was doing a scene in which he was meant to cry, for example, and was having a difficult time crying, he might do his sensory work with his personal object—say, his childhood teddy bear, feeling its weight, smelling its smell, retracing its texture—and the desired emotional reaction would occur. It may sound like some kind of pseudo-psychological voodoo but, practiced over time, it is as reliable as rain.

I called Terry and asked for help. Brookes happened to be at her home and, upon hearing my dilemma, suggested that if I couldn't get rid of the camera from my consciousness, I could turn it into something trusted and safe, something comforting from my past. I instantly thought of my first dog, Duchess.

*That's me in the stylish overall shorts. Duchess in the fur
(and my mom and Peter).*

That night, in my generic, "business traveler" hotel room, I sat in a chair, closed my eyes, and reached out to pet my beloved Airedale. Within moments I felt my shoulders drop and I began to smile. The next day I walked onto the set and approached the camera. Not wanting everyone to think me completely insane, I masked my actions. Gently touching the camera, almost petting it, I asked, "What's this part of the camera do?" and "Is this the lens?"

There was no magic involved: the camera was just a lifeless

machine, possessing no power that I didn't endow it with, so why not endow it with something warm and welcoming instead of something judgmental and harsh? On that day it began to lose its ominous quality. The transformation wasn't instant or total, but it gave me some feeling of control over my fate, which helped me to relax—which was all I was after.

Once I had removed the burden from the camera, I began to get interested in the device itself. What were the different lenses for, how did they work, when was each used, and why? Over time I began to understand that it was not simply what happened in front of the camera that mattered; it was what the camera captured. It may seem a distinction of semantics, but it's not. The finest film acting is often a union of actor and camera. Moments when knowing that a slight lean to the left will cast a shadow on your face that will create the desired emotional effect can be both thrilling and highly effective.

But all that was far too subtle for me at this early stage. I had to settle for not throwing up in front of the camera, and making it into my beloved Duchess was a start.

From the beginning, the movie was out of balance. Lewis, the director, was a sensitive man whose aim was to make a coming-of-age tale in the vein of *The Graduate* meets *The Catcher in the Rye*. The producer, Marty, was hoping to catch the wave of crass teen sex romps that had recently proven big box office. The writers, two funny and ambitious guys named Jim Kouf and David Greenwalt, existed somewhere in between the two poles, but they certainly wanted their jokes to land. While Rob was intuitively wise in charming his path through the minefield of differing creative visions, I agreed with Lewis's more emotionally serious position and sided with him in all matters. It was the first of what would become a career-hampering, almost active refusal to be political in any way.

A savvy older gentleman on the show, an accountant named Michael who dressed only and entirely in black, befriended me along the way and one day pulled me aside. "Marty makes a lot of movies; Lewis makes very few," he said to me. "At this point, you will only ever work for Lewis again."

Worrying, as usual. (That's Alan Ruck and John Cusack in the background.)

I took his meaning, but there seemed little I could do about it. With nothing to hold on to, I clung to what I perceived as the legitimacy of the work. Commercial concerns struck me as mercenary and transactional, reminding me of the mucky waters in which my father swam, and caused me anxiety from which I recoiled.

Near the end of filming, I went to see Michael in his office and confided in him that I felt I had blown my shot. He nodded his understanding, but it's doubtful I was able to properly articulate my feelings of bewilderment.

But it turns out that success is the great forgiver in the film industry. Several years after *Class*, after Rob and I had appeared in *St. Elmo's Fire* together, Marty asked us to do another film. He told my manager, "I know they hate each other, but what's one more?" I was surprised by Marty's remark, as I was very fond of Rob. We were two very different kinds of people and actors, but I always found Rob charming and sincere, with an uncanny ability to laugh at himself. For a time during *St. Elmo's Fire* I fell into the habit of ironically calling him "Bob," which he responded to with knowing playfulness. One moment during the making of a music video for *St. Elmo's Fire*, I passed Rob's open dressing room door. He was eating a sandwich, staring at his reflection in the mirror as he ate.

"Admiring yourself, Bob?"

At that instant, Joel Schumacher walked past. Overhearing my remark, he quipped, "Wouldn't you?"

No one laughed harder than Rob.

For *Class*, I was paid $15,000. This was only slightly above union minimum and, even in 1982, well below what the lead in a mainstream Hollywood movie would normally have made. I didn't care. I hadn't grown up around a great deal of money, although our physical needs and many desires were easily met. From the little I considered it as a boy, money seemed to be dealt with loosely around my home. I knew nothing of how to handle it and, while obviously happy to receive it, gave it no deep thought. I threw the weekly checks in the drawer of the bedside table in my hotel room and watched them accumulate.

Near the completion of filming, I received a call from my father. I hadn't spoken with my parents much over the course of the shoot, save for the normal Sunday call to my mother. My father rarely if ever called me. But he had run into a cash shortage: Was I able to loan him the entirety of my salary for a few weeks? He'd pay me back by the time I got home. I was frightened by his request. He must be in some kind of real trouble, I concluded, to be asking me this. I worried for my mother. But my father was able to explain it away confidently and couch it as something ordinary and normal. I signed my checks over to him and mailed them off.

In the way a child is only remotely aware that his or her parents' struggles are real, I had been dimly conscious that my father had been straining after money for some time. But I now assumed that stress to be the cause of his distraction during visits to me in the city. But his asking for cash in such a direct manner caught me off guard. Because of pride, or shame, my father allowed himself to be made weak by his request, and in time he would come to resent me for that. Conversely—within the dynamic of our relationship—I was made very real and formidable by his need.

Money would grow to define our relationship, and his hunger for cash would not be satisfied.

Two other things of consequence happened near the end of the shoot. Mary Goldberg of the wild hair, who had been the casting director on the film, suggested that she become my manager. I had no idea what a manager did, but Mary, a no-nonsense New Yorker, was direct, and she seemed to have my interests at heart. And she certainly knew more than I did about how show business worked. We would go on to work together for the next dozen years.

The other thing that happened was Jackie Bisset asked what I was doing after the film was over. I informed her that, at the direction of my new manager, I was going to Los Angeles to find an agent. Where was I staying? The only place I knew was the Chateau Marmont, where I had slept the one night of my initial meeting with her, and it had struck me as musty and slightly sinister.

"Well, then why don't you stay with me?" Jackie said.

"Um."

"You don't know anyone in LA. It can be a lonely place. It'll be a pleasure to host you."

And so, with filming in Chicago wrapped up, I settled into the back bedroom of Jacqueline Bisset's Spanish bungalow in the Hollywood Hills. Jackie's welcome was absolute. Perhaps because the home felt so entirely hers, I never stopped to consider what Alexander thought of me bunking down with them for a time. He simply welcomed me with an obliging shrug and a shot of vodka, the way you might offer a stray cat a bowl of milk. Jackie gave me the code to her front-door alarm (I use the same code for various PINs to this day), and my brief tenure in Beverly Hills as roommate to an international sex symbol movie icon and her Russian defector ballet star boyfriend settled into surreal Hollywood normality.

"It's Bisset, as in 'kiss it.'"

The household would rise at ten. Jackie would come into the kitchen in her white robe and make coffee.

"Eggs, Andrew?"

Later, I would lie by the pool, timing Alexander as he worked himself into a sweaty frenzy jumping rope between regular cigarette breaks on my cue. After such a grueling morning, I would head off for various meetings.

I was too young to rent a car, so Jackie kindly offered to drive me to some of my early meetings. During one interview I was asked how I was navigating the city. I mentioned that Jackie was waiting outside in her vintage Cadillac convertible with the top down. As unfamiliar as I was with the ways of Hollywood, I knew that the agent with whom I was speaking would fall out of his chair.

When Jackie was unavailable, I took the bus around town until she kindly recruited an unemployed young man who owned a beat-up car with no air-conditioning to get me where I needed to go.

Back at the house, Alexander was proud of his homemade vodka, which he stored in the freezer. Jackie didn't care for the stuff, and my taste for alcohol had not yet grown so great that I could stomach his toxic brew. (Alexander died from the effects of chronic alcoholism a little more than a decade later.)

There were occasional dinner parties at Jackie's, attended by an international mix. Some I recognized; others I thought I should. I mostly kept my mouth shut so as not to embarrass myself or Jackie, who went out of her way to include me; I was always the youngest in the room by at least a decade. At one party a writer named Zalman King tried to convince Jackie to appear in his screenplay about a couple bound by sexual obsession. It was later made into a movie with Mickey Rourke and Kim Basinger called *9½ Weeks*. After dinner, various African instruments sometimes appeared and might be pounded or scraped.

One afternoon I was lying on the deep green carpet in the den. I was staring up at a large black-and-white photo of Jackie taken during the filming of *Day for Night*. In it she was turning quickly to look over her shoulder, her gaze directly into the lens, her hair wild and blowing, her lips parted slightly, her eyes alive and engaged. It was a gorgeous photograph and the only thing in the house that gave any indication that this was the home of a movie star. Jackie suddenly appeared in the doorway beside the photo.

She asked what I was doing.

"I was looking at your photo," I replied simply.

At which point Jackie came into the room, got on her knees, bent down, and kissed me, deeply.

Just the once.

A few weeks later, as everyone was leaving after another dinner party, Jackie asked me to blow out the candles in the candelabra on her long antique wood table. She went off to get ready for bed. I gave a mighty puff and blew them all out in one breath. In doing so I sent molten wax all over the table. Panicked, I quietly began scraping the fast-drying wax from between the grains on the table. Jackie walked in. I could see the shock on her face, and the flash of stifled anger. Without saying anything, she bent over the table and together in silence we spent the next half hour scraping the table clean. Halfway into our work, Jackie spoke: "It's okay, Andrew." Then she smiled at me. "You didn't know."

There was so much I didn't know.

My return to New York was a jolt. The simple reality was that I had nothing to go back to. Any structure I had loosely clung to (or resisted) had been removed. NYU got wind of my good fortune and offered to let me return, using my semester filming a Hollywood movie as a form of independent study—as long as I paid the tuition, which would have been more than my salary. I thought it was a step backward—and cynical on their part. I never considered it and never mentioned it to my parents.

But where I had been surrounded by classmates, there was now a void, save for Carol, who continued to exert an ongoing and loving influence in my life. Not having been the person voted most likely to get into the movies first, I felt that the few former classmates whom I saw upon my return resented my sudden good fortune. I had stolen a big piece of a small pie, leaving less for them. Whether this was true or solely my perception, it was how I read the situation. I slipped quietly away from contact with most people from school and never looked back, beginning a pattern in my life in which very few of my close friends over the years would be actors.

Yet I didn't know where to place myself. I was in a limbo between professional and student. I continued to study in Terry's Saturday class but felt more and more like an outsider, doing less and less work there. It felt to me both too late and as if I had not yet begun.

And I started going to auditions. Early on, I was excited to get a call about possibly replacing an actor in a Broadway show called *"Master Harold"... and the Boys* by the South African playwright Athol Fugard. It was a lyrical play about the emergence of hatred in a young man during the apartheid era in South Africa. I had seen the play and loved it, although the political nuances were beyond my comprehension.

Fugard, who was also directing, sat halfway back in the empty house of the Lyceum Theatre as I walked out onto a Broadway stage for the first time. I positioned myself behind a large piece of stage set, making me all but invisible from the audience, and began. My voice was thin and weak, swallowed by the vast space. After I read a bit of the scene, Fugard stopped me. Approaching the stage, he asked if I understood something in the material.

I didn't but began to defend myself. "I'm not sure if I have the *right* way to do it, but—"

"There's no right way," he said, gently chiding. He offered up a suggestion, then returned to the second row and sat staring up at me. I ducked farther behind the furniture onstage, mumbled my way through the scene again, and was mercifully dismissed. A hundred similar auditions followed.

Then, six months after completion of the shooting on *Class*, a call came that they wanted to do an additional scene for the end of the movie. Rob was shooting a film in Toronto and we would need to go there for our day of filming. I was envious that Rob had moved on to another big job, while I was floundering. I boarded the plane at a low ebb.

I was seated next to someone who looked familiar. As the plane took off she slept, and I studied the face of the woman whom I'd seen perform in the second act of *Agnes of God* on Broadway several times and even approached one night on the street after the show. When she woke, I was bold with Amanda Plummer for the second time. She was on her way to Toronto to work in the same movie as Rob, *The Hotel New Hampshire*.

We had been placed at the same hotel—not as unlikely as it might sound. Toronto in those days was still a small town, and everyone in the film industry stayed at the Sutton Place. We agreed to meet later that evening.

Amanda and I had a drink in the bar. Then another. I grew smitten—not by Amanda so much as by the idea that someone whom I saw as talented and successful would regard me as a peer. I got only a few hours of sleep before I reported to work hungover. I was unprepared for the day ahead. It marked the first time I would arrive at work in such a condition.

With my friend Amanda.

My task on set was simple enough and yet it proved my undoing. I was to open a door, see Rob standing just behind the camera, say a line to him, and then walk directly toward him past the camera, all the while maintaining eye contact.

I couldn't do it. I opened the door—that part was fine— and I could remember the line without a problem, but I could not keep my gaze from falling to the ground as I walked forward toward the camera. It was as if the camera were able to see into me. The shame I felt from staying out all night, then showing up for work unprepared and hungover, overwhelmed me. I had to look away. There was no way I was going to be able to transform the camera into my loving dog on this day. We did take after take after take. Rob tried to help, teasing me and then staring at me from off camera, trying to will eye contact. Lewis, who had been infinite in his patience with me during the bulk of the filming, grew visibly frustrated. There is no normal number of takes—it depends on the shot—but on something as simple as this, usually a few will suffice. Yet, as the count climbed higher and higher, I grew more and more ashamed. It felt as if I were being tortured. When we reached fifty takes, Lewis stopped.

Despite the fallout from our first meeting, Amanda and I went on to form an enduring friendship. A few years after our Toronto escapade, I was able to convince her to appear in an off-off-Broadway play with me, the first one-act play by a young playwright named Richard Greenberg. The play began with a new song: "Girls Just Want to Have Fun," by an up-and-coming singer named Cyndi Lauper. Over the ensuing thirty years I have never been able to hear it without picturing myself backstage at the "places" call, looking across to the wings on stage left, the only one who could see Amanda break into a few moments of exultant dance each night as the synthesizer splashed in and the lights went to black.

Like me, Amanda was a vintage movie aficionado, and she filled a hole in my cinematic universe when she introduced me to Montgomery Clift. At that particular moment in my development, his work was a revelation. I bought a VCR solely to watch his films again and again. There was a scene in one of his lesser movies, a Vittorio De Sica film called *Terminal Station* (reedited and retitled for American audiences as *Indiscretion of an American Wife*), that I watched hundreds of times.

In the scene, Clift has just put his lover, Jennifer Jones, on a train and he walks back down the platform, the camera tracking along with his movements. Gently, the overcoat he is carrying slips from his hand and begins to drag on the ground.

Lewis trying to set me straight in the production office.

Without looking, in one graceful movement, Clift lifts and folds the coat back over his arm and continues walking—out of frame and on with his life. And the film ends. When I showed the scene to friends, they shrugged, but the simplicity, the metaphorical significance for the character, and the elegance of this mundane, seemingly throwaway gesture screamed out to me. This was the kind of subtle, restrained yet dramatic, almost poetic, and truthful film acting I wanted to do. I now had my cinematic hero. I would begin to dig deeper into script analysis as Clift had done. I would adopt Clift's attitude of East Coast disdain for Hollywood as justification for my own reticence. And Clift's well-documented, self-destructive drinking would be used as additional rationalization for my own incipient problem.

Coinciding with the release of our film, Rob and I were sent on a several-city promotional tour. We went on local morning talk shows, spoke to newspapers, and had a lot of photos taken. Often we were positioned in front of the poster for the film, which consisted of an artist's depiction of Jackie seated on a couch, flanked snugly by Rob in his school uniform and me dressed only in a tie and what I assume was supposed to be a lusty expression. While this was odd enough, the body they had painted for me was that of a buff gym rat, not the scrawny toothpick I was.

In front of my billboard on the Sunset Strip.

It might have been a good idea for someone in the publicity department to give me some kind of media training beforehand or to prepare me in some way for what was expected. Rob and I did most of our interviews together. The dynamic established in our first meeting back at Water Tower Place in Chicago prevailed. Rob was relaxed and happy to chat, not at all embarrassed to speak of his accomplishments. He was received with enthusiasm and made it easy on everyone. My answers tended to ramble and then fizzle, if I could get started at all. I had never heard the term "sound bite." On one morning talk show in San Francisco, I stammered and sputtered so badly that the host finally touched my arm and advised I sit still and try to catch my breath, while Rob leapt in with one more story about the insights gained working with such extraordinary artists as Francis Ford Coppola and Tony Richardson. Not to put too fine a point on it, but I was a lousy interview.

Once, when I was a small child, while my family waited for a table in the Geiger's Cider Mill restaurant, I boasted to my mother, "I'm a pessimist." (I think I had just learned the term.)

"Why, sweetheart?" she asked.

"That way I won't be disappointed if things don't work out."

Despite my own secret hopes for wild success, I carried a similar attitude into the film's release.

When *Class* opened in July of 1983, I was twenty years old. I went and stood in front of the Waverly Theater on Sixth Avenue, a block from Washington Square Park, just a few minutes' walk from my apartment. I looked up and saw the name of the movie on the marquee. Above it a red banner with the film's title slapped in the breeze. The poster with my likeness and name hung in the display window.

I felt as if I were looking at someone else. Even in this first solitary instance, standing by myself on the curb as traffic raced past me up Sixth Avenue, the suddenly public nature of my work did not sit easily with me.

My acting teacher Terry Hayden went to the film and insisted I sit through it with her. Ever candid, she was modest in her praise and pointed out areas where I carried tension. The movie received generally terrible reviews, nearly all of them citing what we had experienced on set: the disconnect between teen high jinks and the attempts at emotional depth. It did scant business.

So now I had done a movie. It had come out. Nothing happened.

Stepping into It

ONE OFT-REPEATED LAMENT is that when in possession of a job, the actor has purpose, a sense of self, and is more or less contented. Without one he is like a marionette with no one holding the strings. He slumps lifeless, waiting. Time slips away, he languishes, an increasingly desperate malaise befalls him. All of which is essentially true. Self-motivation is both a challenge and a must. Which is why actors generally do one of three things (or a combination of all three) when unemployed: they go to the gym obsessively, they go to therapy (obsessively), or they drink (obsessively).

I was not one to commune with the weights, therapy was still a few years away, and my drinking had yet to flash the serious warning signs that would be undeniable in several years' time. I had moved back in with Tommy on Bank Street, but soon word arrived out of the ether from Eddie. He was returning from Thailand and would be needing his old room back.

I moved a few blocks away to West Twelfth Street and Hudson Street in the far west of Greenwich Village. It was across the street from tiny Abingdon Square Park, which was cluttered with discarded hypodermic needles. The dark and nefarious Meatpacking District was a few blocks north. My small one-bedroom affair was on the top floor of a petite three-story corner building containing only four apartments. The floor sloped so drastically I couldn't leave anything on wheels anywhere without it quickly ending up by the front door. It had a fireplace that was technically operational but filled the apartment with smoke if it was lit. I had no furnishings and considered myself lucky when I found a queen-size mattress on the street. I didn't think twice about dragging it up and sleeping on it for the next three years. I got a ten-inch TV. Since all I watched was black-and-white movies, I purchased a black-and-white one. I also got hold of a telephone answering machine that my brother Peter teased me about: Was I so in demand that I would need an answering machine? (I was not in any demand at all, but I still had hopes.) And, most important of all, I was alone. It had never occurred to me that I wanted to live alone, but the instant I was living by myself, I felt at home in a way I never had in my life. The place was a dump, and it was all mine.

I sat on the single section of a modular couch I salvaged from my neighbor and took stock. My movie had come out and was a flop. I had no school to ground me. I was not a part of any community. If, back in high school, it had been my secret plan to attend college for two years and then get into the movies, there was no plan now. I was twenty years old and starting over.

More than a year after *Class* finished shooting, I had yet to find more work. Eddie liked to remark that I had "won the lottery" in getting my first job. It was a comment I always rejected, one that stung, but one that I casually shrugged off. I had been wildly fortunate, no doubt, but I liked to think that in my own way I had been, as E. B. White wrote, "prepared to be lucky." And I was not going to let it all go so easily. I saw acting as my lifeline to who I felt myself to be. But auditions were now more intermittent. I had canceled several recent ones because I just couldn't muster the heart to go, and I had a growing suspicion that my manager, Mary, was beginning to lose faith as well.

I got a call to go in on a commercial. In the 1980s, doing a TV spot was considered far beneath a real actor, just as doing a television series was considered the absolute end of a film career. But I had no career to protect and, as my father had yet to repay any of what I had loaned him, I had little money. I was sick at home with a fever, but fearing that one more canceled audition might be my last, I got out of bed.

I was cast as the Pepsi Boy. The grand concept for the commercial was a play on Americana. The Burger King Girl (dressed in the brown-and-yellow Burger King outfit) and the Pepsi Boy (clad in the classic Pepsi blue-and-white candy stripe) sat close on the stoop of a Norman Rockwell–type front porch, flirtatiously rejoicing that they had finally found each other: "Two winning tastes, together at last."

Together at last... not quite.

When I arrived on the set, we rehearsed and then were sent away. While I was in the makeup trailer, one of the producers came in to speak with the woman applying the light blush to my cheeks. He whispered something into her ear. She nodded gravely, put down the blush, and picked up a robust base. As I went to put on my candy stripe Pepsi shirt, I was given a thick, bulky pad to put on underneath. This was in order to fill out my slight frame, I assumed; no one ever explained the reason to me. I began to question why they had hired me and figured they were doing the same as we did take after take, each one remarkably similar to the last. The single saving grace was the Burger King Girl. Someone in the advertising department had the wherewithal to hire Elisabeth Shue, who would go on to be nominated for an Academy Award some years later for *Leaving Las Vegas*. I developed an instant crush on Elisabeth.

With the day's work done and the commercial complete, I invited her out—and was surprised when she agreed.

In an effort to appear world-weary and wise in hopes of impressing Elisabeth, I took her to the dark and boozy Corner Bistro, where I had a drink too many. A bright light of youthful optimism, she endured my jaded pronouncements—and the drunks surrounding us—as long as she could and then was gone. I never saw Elisabeth again.

I recently mentioned this long-forgotten job to my son, who found it on YouTube. As an actor, ancient embarrassments are always just a click away—but Elisabeth was as adorable as I remembered.

While the commercial didn't do much to advance my nascent career, I was able to pay back some friendly loans and live off the residuals for months, until I got my next job.

Afterschool Specials were exactly what they sound like: aired on a weekday afternoon and aimed at a young audience. They dealt with weighty issues confronting young people: teen pregnancy, parental divorce, smoking. They were idealistic and ultimately uplifting. They have vanished from the landscape.

Eventually called *The Beniker Gang*, this one was about an unlikely group of orphans who escaped their circumstances to form their own family. I was cast to play the leader of this pack of misfits, who also happened to write an anonymous advice column in the local newspaper, naturally. It was directed by Ken Kwapis, a talented young man just a few years older than myself. I felt an instant kinship with Ken, who went on to have an eclectic and successful career, directing

The Office on TV and movies such as *The Sisterhood of the Traveling Pants.*

With Ken (and Charlie Fields).

There was very little money for our modest movie, and we shot in the winter, primarily in an abandoned house that was without heat. We all shivered and huddled around a single small electric heater. I had been so hungry to invest in a project, and under Ken's sensitive hand we felt that what we were doing had meaning. Given the tiny scale and minimal stakes, I felt less intimidated and more in control than I had on my first film...until the big finale, when I had a long and (hopefully) rousing courtroom speech to a judge explaining why he should not break up our improvised family.

The scene was to be shot over two days. On the first afternoon

I was pressing too hard for emotion, unable to relax. I wasn't slated to do my big bit on camera until the second day. That night I went home and, desperate to get my big moment right, called for help. I thought first of Terry Hayden, my acting teacher, but she was always more interested in the process than the result. What I needed was a fix—immediately. I reached out to an acting teacher I knew who had studied with Terry and Strasberg; his name was Tony Greco. Tony was a neurotic, verbal, and perceptive young teacher. I explained my need. He jumped in swiftly and over the phone gave me enough confidence to show up the next day. Tony's help over the next few years, particularly for *St. Elmo's Fire*, would prove invaluable.

Ken began by shooting the close-up of the judge first while I delivered my long and impassioned speech off camera. This is one of the more consequential and glossed-over aspects of filmmaking: which actor gets shot first.

Generally a wide shot is done of the whole scene, with all the actors appearing together on-screen. Once this is complete, each of the actors is more or less photographed individually. In a large scene with several people to be covered, each one requires perhaps five or six takes, plus rehearsals. By the time it gets to your turn, you may have already done the scene thirty or forty times; spontaneity and freshness are long gone. But going later in the process can also be an advantage, giving you time to feed off the other actors' work and figure out what the hell you're doing. And in this case it gave me a chance to gain confidence in what I had prepared. I might cringe if I were to see the scene today, but I relaxed enough so that I was able to deliver what felt like my first legitimate bit of film acting. I was able to execute my work and seize a moment that needed to be seized.

In my first film, I felt that Lewis Carlino and others were fond of me and considered me somewhat talented, but I was so green as to be almost unformed. By my second effort I had begun to take a kind of shape, and Ken's support and his operating assumption that I was up to the task were enough to clear space for me. It allowed my waning belief in myself to reverse its downward spiral and propel me to my next job.

The movie was called *Catholic Boys*. Prior to release it was renamed *Heaven Help Us*, a juvenile title that perfectly captured everything the studio and publicity department got wrong about the movie. Similar to how they hadn't known how to handle *Class* (in fairness, neither had the filmmakers), the publicity department (Tri-Star, in this case) attempted to shoehorn a sad, lonely coming-of-age story about an orphaned teen who was sent to parochial school in Brooklyn in 1965 into "*Porky's* goes to Catholic School." Of course, this type of thinking was, and remains, standard operating procedure in Hollywood. *Porky's* had recently been a wildly successful crass teen sex-capade that cost less than $5 million to make and went on to gross more than $100 million and spawn two sequels. The thinking naturally followed: if that's what the punters want, let's give it to them again, and again, in only slightly repackaged forms.

The problem in this case was that a few masturbation jokes could not mask a more poignant narrative. That the marketing and timing failed to generate the right kind of audience doesn't mean the movie didn't satisfy those few who saw it. To this day a certain type of man who endured Catholic boys' school will approach me on the street; he might stand and block my path, then simply extend his hand in solidarity and mention the title. Others will merely nod their heads with the knowing look of survivors for whom further words are unnecessary. While not remotely the most successful of the films I made in the '80s, *Heaven Help Us* remains my favorite. Not that the making of it was particularly smooth: prior to shooting, we were set for a week of rehearsal; after just a couple of days, the young lead actress was fired.

A few days later, after a morning of rehearsal around the table, I was asked to come back in the afternoon to read with a few of the new candidates for the part. The goal was to see if we fit well together—what I would learn was called a "chemistry read."

John Heard was a sympathetic actor and well cast as the lone empathetic monk in the film. He and Jay Patterson, a humble and earnest man who was to portray the evil Brother Constance, invited me to lunch. I was thrilled to tag along with these older cast members whom I respected. We went around the corner to a Japanese restaurant on Forty-Fifth Street. I had never been to a Japanese restaurant. We sat in the back. John and Jay, who had finished work for the day, ordered sake. A few small, vase like white bottles and tiny porcelain cups arrived at the table.

"Mmmm," each man purred when he took a sip. It all looked harmless enough. I asked for a serving as well. It was warm going down, and strong. I had a vague feeling that I probably shouldn't finish my drink. Then I ordered another. Then I was drunk.

I stumbled back to the office, where I was to read with the actresses hoping for their big break. After the first audition, the director, a young man named Michael Dinner, pulled me aside.

"Have you been drinking?" he asked.

I told him that I had gone out with John and Jay and explained what had happened. He sent me home.

The next morning I was summoned into Michael's office. He asked again what had happened and warned me that such a thing would not be tolerated again. I was deeply embarrassed. I was also more than a little bewildered as to why, after I knew the sake was beginning to affect me at the restaurant, I hadn't stopped.

One of the predominant aspects of alcohol abuse is the baffling power it exerts over its victims. While someone else might have heeded this early warning sign of potential trouble on the horizon, I ignored the implications and instead focused on the more immediate problem of damage control.

I looked across the desk in the windowless office at Michael and said, "I was afraid you were going to fire me." While ashamed about what had happened, I was saying what I knew I should say in such a circumstance to show contrition. I wasn't really afraid of being fired, but maybe I should have been. Perhaps it would have taught me a valuable lesson, although I doubt it. But somewhere inside I knew this was my movie, my stepping-stone, and it was not going to slip away.

A young actress named Mary Stuart Masterson was cast without any help from me. Her combination of privileged tomboy and guarded eagerness proved an ideal foil for my solitary, wary earnestness.

Late in the shoot we were in Coney Island, the faded amusement park by the sea. It was a place my mother had frequented as a child, a place she spoke wistfully about—the parachute ride and the Cyclone, walking down the boardwalk with cotton candy. I had never been there. It was the first warm summer day of late spring. The sky was cloudless. As school was still in session, the place was nearly deserted. Like all seaside retreats out of season, Coney Island had a lonely, melancholy atmosphere that hung close, its ghosts easy to feel. The mood suited our work and my temperament just fine, and in a distant way reminded me of the arcade my mother had taken me to as a small child—where a similar feeling of singular contentment hung over the day.

Our characters sought privacy in the sand under the boardwalk and kissed for the first time. Later we slow-danced to Otis Redding singing, "I've Been Loving You Too Long" from a jukebox in an empty boardwalk snack bar—two lonely young characters with old souls finding comfort and connection in the world for the first time.

Perhaps it was the veil of protection afforded by work that invited such tenderness without risk of consequence, or maybe it was Coney Island summoning some fleeting bit of magic, but I felt I had caught a glimpse of my mother's own lonely youth that afternoon.

Some days were memorable for other reasons. In one scene, my character was being blamed by the evil Brother Constance—my friend Jay—for something I hadn't done and wouldn't say who had. He called me to the front of the class, extracted a large wooden paddle from his desk, then instructed me to put out my hands, palms up, at which point he brought the paddle to bear with full force. The prop department had prepared a foam paddle, but it bent and looked silly each time I was struck. It was quickly discarded in favor of the real thing.

With Mary Stuart Masterson, messing around between takes at Coney Island.

Between each ferocious whack, Jay would ask again for the name I refused to give up.

The director had an image in his mind. There is a moment in the film *The Elephant Man* when Anthony Hopkins lays eyes on the title character for the first time. The camera slowly pushes in on Hopkins, who stands motionless as a single tear rolls down his cheek. Michael wanted to create a similar moment as my hands were repeatedly hammered. But the force of the blows with the real paddle was so extreme that I recoiled on contact, my face contorted in anguish as I stared back in defiance at Jay. Instead of that single graceful drop, tears sprang from my eyes, which grew redder and more swollen with each ensuing take. Michael pressed on, doing take after take, hoping for a simpler reaction. Eventually he accepted the scene as it was. It remains a powerful and raw moment, but as a young actor I had no idea how to protect myself. My hands were deeply bruised and swollen for weeks after. And I walked away feeling I had failed, knowing the director had desired the more stoic response.

There were others times when I had difficulty with Michael as well. He had done an elegant, disturbing version of *Miss Lonelyhearts* starring Eric Roberts at the American Film Institute. Ours was his first feature film. He went on to be very successful in television, producing and directing many popular shows. I've run into him over the years and he has always been gracious, yet as a young man I felt on some level that he didn't care for me. As a defense against feeling that I couldn't satisfy him, and in an effort to gain back some feeling of control, when Michael directed me I would often get angry and become unable to focus on what he was asking of me. I knew I didn't have this luxury. I reached out again to Tony Greco, who had helped me in a pinch during *The Beniker Gang*. He suggested I simply clap my hands once whenever the director did anything that irritated me, and in doing so my aggression would find release.

From then on, when Michael asked me to move left and I wanted to go right, I simply clapped my hands in a gentle way and went left without resentment.

"Can you be sadder?"

CLAP.

"Sure."

"Can you do that faster?"

CLAP.

"No problem."

I'm not sure if Michael ever noticed my little tic, but it got me through. And in fairness to Michael, he fought—and in most ways succeeded—to make the movie that both he and the writer, a brooding, slightly tortured soul named Charlie Purpura, wanted to make.

My orphaned character in *Heaven Help Us* lived in the home of his alcoholic, TV-watching aunt, played by a Canadian character actress named Kate Reid. Kate worked constantly and had hundreds of jobs over her forty-year career. During our filming she was costarring on Broadway with Dustin Hoffman in *Death of a Salesman*. She invited me to the show, and I went backstage to see her afterward. She took me around to meet Hoffman. Just a few days earlier on the set, during a scene in which a school bus drove past, on impulse I had slapped its side-view mirror with my hand, highlighting my character's frustration in the scene. After the take, the camera operator said to me, "That shtick reminded me of a young Dusty," and I took it as a great compliment. At this time Hoffman was at the top of the heap, an actor's actor. He had won an Academy Award several years earlier for *Kramer vs. Kramer* and was most recently a revelation while cross-dressing in *Tootsie*. To a budding New York actor, meeting Dustin Hoffman at this stage was as close to meeting royalty as I could imagine. Backstage, he could not have been more gracious and solicitous. We talked about the movies and the theater; he talked about the specificity needed in acting choices and the importance of the right shoes for a character. ("They can tell you everything," he confided, as if sharing a family secret.) He treated me as the equal I wasn't. As I was getting up to leave, he grabbed my hand.

"We'll work together," he said with feeling.

I could feel my left eye beginning to twitch. I mumbled, "I would love that," and hurried away.

We have never worked together.

While I never drank sake with John Heard and Jay Patterson again, many nights after shooting I would join them at John's local pub, the All State Café on Seventy-Second Street, west of Broadway. Down four steps, past the phone booth by the door, the bar lined the wall on the right, with tables opposite and farther back. The place was wood-paneled and cave-like. It had a welcoming feel and an infamous New York pedigree. In 1973, Roseann Quinn, a schoolteacher and regular, was murdered by a man she left the bar with and became the inspiration for the book and movie *Looking for Mr. Goodbar*, starring Diane Keaton.

John was well-regarded by the barman and patrons alike and we were welcomed into the clubby atmosphere because of him. Both men drank copiously, and I discovered myself more than able to keep up. I noted this escalation in my drinking without the slightest concern; instead, it felt to me like finally growing up.

On the many mornings after I drank too much, I took to dunking my head into a sink full of ice. I had heard somewhere that Paul Newman used this trick and I began to do the same in my tiny bathroom on West Twelfth Street. I kept it up for the duration of the film; this, too, felt somehow like adulthood.

I was also beginning to cobble together my own way of working. I had by now read a great deal on my cinematic hero Montgomery Clift and learned that he had dissected his lines into very conscious phrasing. I began to scribble notations in the margins of my script, breaking up dialogue, searching for added meaning in particular lines. Clift had been respected both as an actor and as a movie star, and I yearned for the same.

One night during filming, I was at a party at the home of a powerful agent. Jack Nicholson held court on the sofa, but I was more interested in the bookish woman by the buffet: I cornered Patricia Bosworth, who had written a definitive biography of Clift. I'd read it twice. I held her captive and regurgitated much of her book back at her as if offering new insights. "Did you know...?" would start most of my pronouncements. Yes, she did know, having written the book on it. But, backed into a wall, Patricia received my youthful onslaught graciously.

On set I was maturing as well. Since my early experience of making the camera into my beloved dog, I had continued to become more and more interested in the technical aspects of filmmaking. We had an old-school, hard-edged New York crew and a legendary Czech cinematographer named Miroslav Ondrícek. They welcomed my interest. Miroslav walked with a limp and carried a cane and was full of wisdom he was eager to share—on his own terms. One day he laid his cane hard across the back of my legs when he caught me looking through his camera without permission. And Vinnie, the chain-smoking assistant camera operator, whose job was to keep things in front of the lens in focus, offered me some tough love as well after I missed my mark one too many times.

"Andy, you want to be in focus?"

"Yeah, Vinnie."

"Then hit your fucking mark."

It was a different time, and I took it all in the spirit intended. I was an eager apprentice being welcomed into the filmmaking fold. When the camera operator approached me near the end of the shoot and said, "You became a pro on this one, Andy," you could have knocked me over with a feather.

Igniting It

FOR SOME REASON Robert Redford took a liking to me. Redford, of course, resides in the pantheon of film gods. At this point, in 1985, he had recently won an Academy Award for directing *Ordinary People*, but his status as an American icon dated back to *Butch Cassidy and the Sundance Kid*. I was twenty-one.

I'd been invited up to the Sundance Institute for its annual June lab, in which young filmmakers were brought in to workshop their scripts. Veteran directors and writers came by the dozen to mentor them, and actors were needed to fill the roles. All this was Redford's vision; he created it out of nothing, on land he owned in the mountains of Utah. It was filmmaking sleepaway camp for the famous and up-and-coming— well before Sundance became the juggernaut it is today. (The renowned film festival was still a small-town affair called the U.S. Film Festival.)

I was assigned to work on a script by a new writer-director named Michael Hoffman, along with a young actress named

126

With my early hero and Laura Dern at Sundance.

Laura Dern. Redford, as well as directors like Sydney Pollack and George Roy Hill, might stop in to watch the work and comment.

One day at lunch, Redford took me aside. "Why don't you come up to the house sometime?"

"Uh, okay."

On one corner of the desk in his office was a discreet stack of magazines with Redford's likeness on the covers. (Years later, for a brief time, I did the same with magazines in which my travel writing appeared.) He spoke to me of alternating the studio movies he did with more independent fare like *Jeremiah Johnson*, which he had filmed on his land. Redford made me feel that I had something special to offer and was worth his time. Why he went out of his way, I never knew, but it went a long distance toward boosting my confidence as I headed west for what I knew was my biggest job to date.

Early on, when I was struggling to get any job, I auditioned for a ridiculous movie called *D.C. Cab*, a star vehicle for Mr. T. The director was a tall, rakish man named Joel Schumacher. I met Joel to read for the young lead character. The audition went nowhere and I never thought twice about it. When the movie came out a year later, I didn't go to see it but was glad I wasn't in it.

Then I received a call. Joel was directing a new movie. He had remembered my audition for *D.C. Cab* and wondered if I would come read for his new film. It was called *St. Elmo's Fire*, the story of a group of friends on the cusp of adulthood after just graduating Georgetown University. Joel wanted me to read for the role of the prematurely jaded, aspiring writer named Kevin. I did, and quickly became Joel's choice. But there was resistance from the studio to casting me: I had yet to appear in a successful movie and had no name recognition. At the time, I was unaware that any of this mattered; in fact, I was unaware of nearly all aspects of the business end of the film industry. As far as I knew, if the director wanted you for the part, you got the part. Not so.

I was flown out to Los Angeles and put up at the Chateau Marmont, just as I had been when I was brought out to meet Jacqueline Bisset for *Class*. This time things did not go as smoothly. It started well enough: a stretch limousine was sent to fetch me. The oversize SUV as means of celebrity transport was still decades away, and the stretch limo was the ultimate in Hollywood status. I was taken over the hill to Burbank, where

Warner Bros. and Columbia Pictures shared soundstages and the back lot. Initially excited as I hopped into the black car, I soon began to grow nervous about the impending meeting. I became so uncomfortable in the back of the giant vehicle that, at a red light, I got out and went around to sit up front beside the very surprised driver. It was a practice I kept up for a few years, causing no end of confusion and discomfort for unsuspecting chauffeurs.

Once at the studio—after the obligatory ten-minute wait prior to all meetings in Hollywood in which the more powerful person exerts his dominion by keeping the less powerful party waiting a noticeable but not rudely excessive amount of time— I was brought in to meet Craig Baumgarten, executive vice president of Columbia Pictures. No one had told me exactly what the purpose of the meeting was, but I intuitively knew I was there to impress. This pretext embarrassed me and struck me as manufactured and false. Joel was there as well. In his charming, outgoing manner, he tried to get conversation going.

"I first met Andrew for *D.C. Cab.* He was too good for it. [*Laughs.*] But he stuck in my mind. Right, Andrew?"

"Uh-huh."

"Did you ever see the movie?" Craig asked me, laughing along.

"Nope." [*Not laughing.*]

Beside me on the couch, Joel not so playfully slapped me on my shoulder, trying to rouse me to the challenge. He could do little as I slouched farther down, saying next to nothing, demonstrating no interest in the conversation or the film I was there to get cast in. Even as I knew I was tanking the meeting, I sank behind a feeling of helpless self-consciousness.

"You enjoy coming to LA, Andy?" Craig kept trying.

"Not really."

I was soon dismissed. Slouching out of the room, I heard Joel call from over my shoulder to his assistant, a big, gentle guy named Paul Kaplansky.

"Give Andrew a lift back. And then get right back here."

We squeezed into his Volkswagen Beetle and started back over the hill. In Los Angeles, what you drive says everything about you, and the fact of my returning in the most humble of cars, after arriving in the grandest ride, suddenly struck me. In a rush, I told Paul my true feelings: that I loved the part and how much I wanted to be in the movie.

"Well, then why didn't you act like it?" he asked as he swerved his Beetle up Coldwater Canyon.

My feigning disinterest was by now simply my go-to defensive reaction, one that would take me years to unravel and name as fear. All I knew at the time was that I had blown it. "Please," I begged Paul, "please tell Joel how much I want to do the movie." Paul said he'd try and let me out in front of my hotel.

Paul did talk to Joel. Joel called and scolded me, then went to the mat for me.

Leading up to the movie, I had what seems a silly fear, but one that spoke to a deeper worry. Up to then I had played only high school students, and because I still looked so young, I was worried that no one would believe me in the role of a college graduate. A friend pointed out that I was exactly the right age and would have been a graduate myself if I had made it that far in my education. That worry vanished, but it revealed what was underneath. Was I mature enough to create the character I was after?

Actors often find it easier to perform a part that is very far removed from their nature. An accent can be liberating; the nicest guy in the world can find great freedom in playing a monster. Parts that hit closer to home can prove elusive. The character of Kevin was very much like me, and I knew what made him behave the way he did. I believed, for the first time, that I could do the part better than anyone else. What I understood was that, beneath his casual disregard, his rotten-before-it's-ripe cynicism, there was a depth of feeling that ached for connection. I wanted to illuminate that. What I needed was something I could rely on when inspiration failed.

Once again I called on Tony Greco, who had been so helpful when I was in a pinch with *The Beniker Gang* and *Heaven Help Us*. If Kevin's dominant characteristic was defensive sarcasm, then it stood to reason that he was covering a well of vulnerability, just as most people who employ such defenses are. The key was to turn up the volume on the suppressed vulnerabilities so that Kevin did not simply appear as a defensive jerk but as the wounded, frail animal he was, worthy of friendship and love. What was needed was a loud subtext screaming to those he loved to come closer, a subtext that could be heard through each sarcastic and distancing comment. Tony and I simply set about amplifying my own vast vulnerabilities. The logic went that if I felt so exposed, I would naturally cover those feelings in a defense I was already well versed in; then the result would be not simply a shell of sarcasm but the human ache underneath coming through loud and clear.

The work would be in how to do it reliably, so that it was accessible to me whenever I needed it. I went back to what Terry had taught me. I began looking for a simple personal object from my childhood, when I had been the most vulnerable—one that I could re-create through the sensory work I had become proficient in. I settled on a stuffed bear that I had received for Christmas when I was seven. It was the first year I knew that my parents actually provided the bounty, and yet I kept that knowledge secret from them as I cooed over what Santa Claus had brought. While I loved the bear, I have always recalled it as symbolizing my first awareness that Santa wasn't real. It became a charged object of lost innocence.

Within a few minutes of tactilely exploring its memory, tears streamed down my face. Then a song my mother used to sing to me as a small child, one I hadn't thought of in years, came to me. It contained strange lyrics for a children's lullaby—about "bums" and "cigarette trees" and "a lake of gin we can both jump in"—but as a child, who pays attention to such things when their mother sings it in a breathy voice filled with tender love?

Each morning thereafter, before work, I sat in a chair for ten minutes and conjured up my teddy bear while humming my mother's lullaby. My defenses dropped and I was quickly in touch with my own frailties and feelings of being alone in the world. The rest of the day all I had to do was cover up that ache I had worked to create in the privacy of my room. It also provided me with a secret—something most interesting performances carry. I was ready to go.

I just had to get comfortable around these strangers who were supposed to be my closest friends. I knew Rob from *Class*, but the rest were new to me. They seemed to all have a history with each other. Rob and Emilio Estevez were close friends. Emilio had been romantic partners with Demi

The St. Elmo's Fire *gang.*

Moore, and he had done a yet-to-be-released movie called *The Breakfast Club* with Judd Nelson and Ally Sheedy. The only other person of the core group who shared no history with the others was Mare Winningham, on whom I developed a deep and abiding crush that would hang over me for several years. Being pregnant at the time of filming and already a mother of two young children, Mare suffered my adoration as patiently as her already full life would allow.

A curious aside peripherally involving Mare happened a year or so earlier, when I met her for the first time. We were both auditioning for a film called *The Sure Thing* that Rob

With Mare.

Reiner was directing, in which John Cusack was eventually cast. Rob had appeared famously as Meathead in *All in the Family* on TV in the '70s and went on to direct such movies as *When Harry Met Sally...* and the hilarious *This Is Spinal Tap*. During auditions, actors were teamed in pairs to read, and I was matched with Mare. The audition was in Rob's hotel room and the reading went well, yet I was told soon after that it was "not going any further" by my manager. I was slightly surprised, considering the reception in the room. Decades later I directed Rob in a television show. He remembered the audition and brought it up to me. "You were great," he said. "When you walked out of the room I was seriously considering casting you, and then suddenly in the hallway I heard you start to whistle, and that was it. I don't know why, but that did it for me. You were out."

Cockiness never suited me.

Before the shoot on *St. Elmo's Fire* was set to begin, we had several days of rehearsal on the studio lot in Los Angeles. It was the first time I had been on a Hollywood soundstage. The vast space was empty save for a few long tables set up under temporary lights. The catwalks of the high ceiling and the padded walls fell into darkness, where it felt to me like the ghosts of past films watched over us. I was early and sat slouched in a folding chair at one corner of the table. The other actors arrived, hugging one another and exchanging high fives. Demi swept in with Joel. We read through the script. There was a slight but unmistakable undercurrent of competition, but I felt everyone was well cast. It seemed there might be a place for me on the periphery of the group, observing, waiting, keeping my own counsel, then chiming in when I felt I could score.

Joel talked openly to the group about Demi recently getting sober. I didn't even know what "getting sober" meant. His words conveyed pride, but in his tone I heard a warning. Demi smiled and nodded her head. In time Demi and I became affectionate in a distant way: she would playfully scold me about being aloof, while I teased her about being "fabulous." Our relationship—like my relationships with most of the cast—mirrored our on-screen dynamics. I was friendly enough with Emilio but we never connected in any real way. I always felt his judgment, as if he belonged to a club I could never join. A few years later we were both asked to do a film about the young men who organized the Woodstock music festival. I was excited by the idea, but Emilio wasn't interested if I was involved. I took it quite personally, but, in fairness to him, this was after the "Brat Pack" moniker had been leveled and Emilio was taking great pains to distance himself from any association with those likewise stigmatized. It hurt my feelings nonetheless, and I don't think the movie ever got made.

I was always affectionately bemused by Rob's self-awareness and career-savvy instincts, while I sensed in Judd an edgy ambition and circled him warily. Ally was her quirky self. She made efforts to bring me into the group. And early on she drove me around in her open-top Jeep. For no good reason, I remember her driving me back to my hotel after rehearsal one day as the wind whipped through the open car. I don't know why I recall the drive, as nothing of consequence transpired, other than we were young and life was beginning to happen for us. Ally's generosity meant a lot to me.

To begin filming, we relocated for a two-week location shoot in Georgetown. Right away, I knew this one was different. During a night scene, my character, Kevin, took a lonely, melancholy walk home and confronted a familiar prostitute on the corner. "How come you never proposition me?" I demanded of her.

"I thought you were gay," she said.

It was a fun, well-written scene. The huge arc lights hoisted high up in the sky on cranes called out for attention; the streets were hosed down to shimmer in the night. Slouching along in my camel-hair overcoat, I felt as if I had been preparing for this moment for years, shuffling around alone so many evenings through the streets of Greenwich Village. Emilio, Rob, and Demi dropped by to watch. I was aware of feeling lucky

Hanging with Rob. At least one of us knew the scene.

and secretly happy. As much as I dared admit it to myself, I knew I was the right person in the right job in the right place at the right time.

Once we returned to Los Angeles, shooting shifted to the studio lot. One evening at wrap, Emilio announced to the boys that he was going to see Sylvester Stallone in the new *Rambo* movie on its opening weekend. I had no desire to see the film but felt I ought to join the group. I met the other three guys in Westwood, where the show was sold out.

"I'll handle this," Emilio said. "Back in a minute."

Rob, Judd, and I waited out on the street while Emilio went off to speak to the theater manager. Within minutes he returned.

"All set," he said, that charming Emilio smirk on his face.

Emilio would employ a similar trick some months later. With a journalist from *New York* magazine tagging along, he finagled a free ticket into another Westwood cinema. The writer interpreted this trick as a sense of entitlement, turned off to his subject, and would soon coin the phrase that would haunt many of us for years to follow.

After the movie, the guys were revved up over the muscles and explosions. I couldn't shake the feeling that they were all experiencing something I wasn't, or perhaps it was the other way around. Regardless, I felt ever the outsider and made a quiet and quick exit. That evening was one of the rare occasions when I went out with any of the guys during filming— with one other notable exception.

On a Friday night after filming, Rob invited me to join him and his girlfriend, the actress Melissa Gilbert of *Little House on the Prairie* fame, at Spago, the hottest eatery on the Sunset Strip. Surprised by the invite, I happily accepted and chased Rob's taillights over Laurel Canyon. I thought it would just be the three of us and maybe a friend of Melissa's, but when we arrived, the table was full. Rob's agent and a few others were present, as well as a woman seated to my right who was introduced to me simply as Liza.

I ordered a double vodka.

More drinks were had and Ms. Minnelli could not have been more charming, her rasping voice and throaty laugh directed as often as not in my direction. As the restaurant was thinning out, Liza suggested we head up to Sammy's. Everyone cooed at the idea. I had no idea what Sammy's was but cooed along with the others. She got up to make a call. When she returned, Liza confirmed we would indeed be welcomed at Sammy's.

I left my car at the restaurant and hopped in with Rob. I had assumed Sammy's was a nightclub. But as we drove deeper up into residential Beverly Hills and then turned into a private driveway behind a large gate, it became clear this was no nightclub we were going to. We all piled out and approached the front door. I had no idea where we were. I was more than half-drunk. I kept my mouth shut. There was a large knocker in the center of a heavy door, which Liza raised and let fall. The door was swung open by a small man who spread his arms wide and shouted, "Cats!"

Sammy Davis Jr. welcomed us into his home. "I'm just finishing screening a flick for some friends; it's almost done," he purred. "Go on upstairs to the billiard room and I'll call you in a few."

As I racked the pool balls upstairs, Rob, who tended not to be flustered by much, turned to me and mouthed, "Holy shit!"

Then Sammy called us down and we joined the party. Sammy, who had stopped drinking some years earlier, played bartender and gracious host. Stationed behind the sunken bar in the corner of his living room, he handed me a large vodka on the rocks.

"I love what you young cats are doing." He winked his good eye and pointed his cigarette at me just as Sammy Davis Jr. might. "I'm watching."

A large fish tank filled the fireplace, and most of Sammy's wall space was covered with 8x10 black-and-white photos of Sammy with various celebrities. Sammy shared inside jokes about a few of the pictures, only I wasn't in on the joke. I laughed along anyway. I had another drink. We shared another cigarette. After a while Sammy excused himself up to bed but urged us to stay and party on as long as we liked. So we did.

Later, Liza insisted on driving me home. We went by

her house to get the keys to her green Rolls-Royce, which she wanted to drive me in. We chatted in her living room. "Mark's upstairs asleep," she whispered. Liza perched on the piano stool, her elbow up on the baby grand. I slouched on the couch, dancing the razor's edge of being too drunk and just drunk enough to relax and enjoy hanging with Liza Minnelli in the middle of the night at her Beverly Hills pad while her husband slept upstairs.

As she drove me back to my sublet, I began to grow nauseous. Fearing I might vomit all over Liza's Rolls, I tried to lower my window. Either it was locked or broken, but it wouldn't budge. In an effort to distract myself, I blurted out that I really enjoyed Willie Nelson's rendition of "Somewhere over the Rainbow," and by the time Liza pulled up to the curb in front of my building we were deep into a discussion of parents—her very famous ones and my not-famous-at-all ones. We talked until the new day had beaten back the darkness. It was a tender, intimate chat—and, like the rest of the evening, simultaneously bizarre and utterly normal. I haven't seen Liza since.

While making *St. Elmo's Fire*, I lived for a few months at the Sunset Marquis, an upscale rock 'n' roll hotel in West Hollywood. It felt as if every major act in music passed through while I was there. Late one night I ended up in a room listening to Annie Lennox hold forth about vocal nodes to Cyndi Lauper. I got drunk with Bob Seger. One of the Go-Go's chased me around the pool (which one I can't recall), but no sightings were more exciting than those of Bruce Springsteen and his band, who were staying there during his *Born in the U.S.A.* tour.

I'd have breakfast on the patio next to the piano player, Roy Bittan. Nils Lofgren quietly strummed the national anthem on an acoustic guitar from his balcony above the pool. In the Boss's bungalow, at one after-show party, I danced to Wilson Pickett's "634-5789" late into the night. There were actors as well: Roy Scheider, in his red Speedo swimsuit, occupied a permanent spot on a reclining chair by the pool, his phone dragged out beside him, its long cord snaking back inside the sliding glass door of his poolside room. One evening I ended up at a party in someone's suite and spotted a cute young woman with a pixie haircut and a happy manner across the room. I chatted her up, but Courteney Cox was having none of me. (This was pre-*Friends*, but—even more impressive to me—she had just appeared in Bruce Springsteen's "Dancing in the Dark" video.) Life was pretty good.

But even rock 'n' roll heaven can grow wearisome. After showing up for work one morning with only a paper-thin grasp of my lines, I knew I needed to refocus. I moved out and into a sublet in a Colonial Revival building designed by Leland A. Bryant on Havenhurst Drive, a few blocks east. It was a generous one-bedroom with French windows and arched hallways that belonged to Carol Kane—among the most wonderfully quirky of quirky actors—who was out of town on a project. Carol had alerted me that my next-door neighbor on the fourth floor, living just on the other side of my wall, was the legendary Bette Davis. Whenever I returned home, I loitered for an instant as I fished out my key to see if perhaps I might encounter the mythic star. Alas, I never saw her. But, all alone, I was safe in Carol's elegant apartment in a way I couldn't be at the hotel, no matter how heady the scene by the pool.

As a welcoming gift to mark the start of filming, the producers had given me a bottle of red wine. For a long while it remained unopened. I had never even drunk wine, but it seems telling to me now that I took the bottle with me from my hotel to my new home. One evening soon after my arrival in my new apartment, feeling adrift and looking to fulfill some romantic notion I had about living a tragic artist's existence, I sat in the window seat, threw open the sash, popped the cork, and took a sip. I didn't care for the astringent taste, but I finished the glass. Then I poured another. Until the bottle was empty. It marked the first time I would drink alone.

Joel Schumacher and I shared an uneasy alliance through filming. One evening, we were shooting in and around the St. Elmo's bar that had been constructed on the back lot of the studio. As we waited for night to fall, Joel took me aside and walked me away from the set. He put his arm around my shoulder as we strolled and proceeded to tell me that I was a great artist. I could feel a "but" coming, and it didn't take long. "Like all great artists," Joel went on, "you are very selfish." He cited no examples of my behavior or how my attitude might have unseated the balance of the unit. With that said, he turned and we returned to work. I never learned what had touched off this conversation, and nothing about my conduct or temperament was ever mentioned again. While I wasn't prepared to argue with Joel's conclusion, I was very confused as to why he had chosen to have this little chat when he did or what its larger purpose was. It felt simply like an opportunity to scold in an attempt to control. At another moment in life I might have allowed such comments to make me wither. But

I felt secure enough—for the first time—in the work I was doing, and continued to simply hold my space despite the unsettling nature of the conversation. Later that evening we were shooting a scene in the bar and I was positioned on the phone as the camera passed by on the way to someone else. I ad-libbed a line into the receiver that has often been quoted back to me over the years: "Me? It ain't easy being me."

In most of my '80s films I had at least one love scene. I was always uncomfortable with these, feeling physically scrawny and too exposed—in both the literal and the emotional sense. The one between Ally and myself was no exception.

It all began without incident. We played out a scene in which I confessed my long-harbored secret love for her, then things got physical. Joel instructed us to make love with ferocious passion on the coffin that served as a coffee table in the living area of the set. We nodded our understanding and went at it. Apparently, Ally and I weren't giving Joel enough of what he wanted, and after multiple takes, his frustration was too much to contain. During the middle of a take Joel screamed out, "You're FUUUUUUCCCCCKKKKKINGGGG!"

Ally burst into tears. I stood up, clad only in a small patch of flesh-colored cover, and yelled back at Joel, "What the hell do you know about making love with a woman anyway!"

Joel stared back at me. I huffed and puffed some more, forgetting my generally unclad state, while the crew stared at their feet.

Everyone eventually settled down and we resumed. Things never got to where I'm certain Joel would have liked them to get, but we moved on to the shower portion of the activities.

Since we were on a soundstage and everything about the set was fake, the running water had to be specially piped in— only they had neglected to make it hot. In a cold shower, we set about trying to create some heat. Joel instructed me to press Ally up against the glass stall door from behind in the show of passion he was still craving. I obliged as best I could, but being a cheaply constructed soundstage set, the shower door came crashing down. The tension broke, we all burst into laughter, and the shot is in the film.

A few days later we were filming on the same set, the apartment that belonged to Emilio's and my characters. In the scene I was alone, singing along to Aretha Franklin's classic "Respect." I was extremely self-conscious about having to sing. One could draw a straight line from my anxiety all the way back to my deliberately poor audition for glee club during middle school, when Mr. Little had implanted in me the notion that I was tone-deaf.

I needed something.

Now, there are two kinds of actors: those who love props and those who hate them. I've met wonderful actors who can't hold a glass of water and act at the same time, and I know some pretty limited ones who can juggle while standing on their heads; it just depends on their internal wiring. For those who dislike props, interaction of any kind with objects can be awkward and intrusive, while for someone like me they were a lifeline. A cup of coffee, or a watering can, or—the queen of all props back then—a cigarette, could help to ground the work and take the internal focus away from the self and place it on behavior, liberating the performance.

During the course of the shoot, I had been reading about

Marlon Brando and learned that he played the bongo drums when he was a young actor. I bought myself a set. Having lousy rhythm, I was lousy on them. I lost interest quickly, and the drums sat in the corner of my room. But as I was walking out to work on the morning the scene was to be filmed, I grabbed them. Joel thought they were a nice touch.

Slapping those bongos, no matter how poorly, liberated me. Suddenly I was flopping around, flinging myself up and down on the bed as I shrieked along with Aretha—a private moment of freedom and joy my character would never allow others to witness. Afterward I felt particularly raw and only half jokingly said to the cameraman, "Well, that should kill my career—not that I had one."

Steve Burum, the director of photography, was standing beside the camera and overheard. Steve was a mild-mannered pro, professorial in appearance. He squinted at me and said, "I'd say you made your career on this one."

And he was right. After the movie came out, everything was different.

—

It's difficult to imagine now, but the movies were not always pitched at an adolescent sensibility. The advent of the talkies in the late 1920s saw Al Jolson in *The Jazz Singer*. The '30s and '40s gave us classic adult entertainment like *Gone with the Wind*, *Citizen Kane*, and *Casablanca*, as well as the rugged Americana of John Ford. The western still rode high in the '50s with *The Searchers*, *Shane*, and *High Noon* but also ushered in the kitchen-sink naturalism of Elia Kazan's *On the Waterfront* and Truffaut's *400 Blows*. Alfred Hitchcock was creating some of his most enduring classics with *North by Northwest, Vertigo,* and *Rear Window*. Then the '60s produced epics like *Lawrence of Arabia* and *Doctor Zhivago,* but also the cool cruelty of *Bonnie and Clyde*. The decade may have started with the moral certainty of *To Kill a Mockingbird,* but it ended with the likes of *The Graduate, Easy Rider,* and *Midnight Cowboy,* reflecting the rudderless quality of a nation adrift. The '70s brought sophisticated, challenging, director-driven entertainment for grown-ups—*The Godfather* (parts one and two), *Alice Doesn't Live Here Anymore, The French Connection, Coming Home, Taxi Driver, Dog Day Afternoon, A Clockwork Orange, All the President's Men, Day for Night, Nashville,* and on and on.

But with the birth of the blockbuster in mid-decade, movies like *Jaws* and *Star Wars* went a long way toward creating a tidal wave of younger audiences. Genre films like *Carrie* and *Halloween,* and musicals such as *Grease,* showed the growing power of the youth market. Late in the decade, *Animal House* came out of nowhere and John Belushi surprised everyone. In the early 1980s the teen romance *Blue Lagoon,* featuring the insane beauty of Brooke Shields, would do huge business, and the aforementioned *Porky's* had the kind of success that Hollywood loves to imitate. The young audience was primed to be exploited in a way that it never had been before. Things were ready to explode—and make the success of young actors like myself possible.

By the mid-1980s, youthful stupidity and sex had been well chronicled, but there was one aspect of adolescence that had not been seriously mined on-screen. Few films had treated the overwhelming, all-consuming power of teenage emotions earnestly, depicted teens with respect for their struggles, or given them a sense of genuine dignity on-screen.

Enter John Hughes.

It strikes me as unlikely that John would have become the voice that illuminated the pains and pangs of youth a generation his junior. Having come from the world of *National Lampoon*, John's early work and many of his later efforts were comedic, bordering on crass in nature. I always thought his relatively brief foray into adolescent angst touched on something deep that resided in John and his past growing up outside Chicago—a sensitivity that was too vulnerable to leave exposed to the world for long—and thus he retreated back behind his facile touch to the broad comedy of *Uncle Buck*, *Home Alone*, and beyond. My dime-store, pop psychology analysis of a man I knew little was based on the one film I did for him. We never shared a meal, I was never invited to his home, and I don't recall him ever asking me a personal question. John struck me as a private, wary guy who guarded his own sensitivities with an affable presence, a fast mind, a quick remark, and an iron will.

Since discovering it in high school, I hadn't considered an option for me other than acting. And since holding my own during *St. Elmo's Fire*, I felt on more solid ground in my choice of career, at least momentarily. That didn't mean I was relieved of the constant anxiety that I would never work again. Exactly when and where my next job might come from was still very much in doubt. A teenage redhead I didn't know at all would see to that problem and facilitate my getting the part that I'm still reminded of on a near-daily basis.

The *Breakfast Club* had recently been released, and with its success coming on the heels of *Sixteen Candles*, both John and Molly Ringwald were in an enviable position. A new type of teen film was emerging and John was the visionary behind it, with Molly as his muse. John's movies had a singular voice, confidence, and sincerity. Molly was equally assured, unique and raw. *Pretty in Pink* was to be their next collaboration. John had written the movie for Molly but he was going to only produce the film, handing the directing chore over to a soft-hearted, self-deprecating New York neurotic named Howard Deutch. All I cared about at this point was that they were coming to New York and, according to my agent, weren't interested in auditioning me. They were looking for a "hunk," a "star quarterback type," to play the rich love interest to Molly's girl from the wrong side of the tracks. I was informed I did not fit the bill.

But with *St. Elmo's Fire* coming out soon, there was a bit of prerelease buzz. In some conversations—primarily the ones initiated by movie publicists—it was being called "the young *Big Chill*," an ensemble film filled with stars a decade older, stars like William Hurt and Kevin Kline. (In fact, when *St. Elmo's Fire* was released a few months later, one reviewer called it "a poor man's *Big Chill*, a day late and a dollar short." At least the publicists had done their job and gotten the two films spoken of in the same sentence.) And because of that chatter about my soon-to-be-released movie (you are never more intriguing than before anyone has seen your work), I was awarded a courtesy audition.

I waited my turn out in the hall. Most of the time actors go into an audition room and read the scene with a casting assistant—usually a well-meaning person and a terrible actor. But in this case Molly was there, seated beside the video camera. At the time, I had not seen any of Molly's films, although it would have been impossible not to recognize her after walking past my newsstand on Sheridan Square and seeing all the magazine covers with her likeness. Behind her, leaning forward, elbows on his knees, perched an eager, dark-haired, and well-intentioned man: the director, Howie. Then in the back of the room, behind the equipment, hands stuffed deep into the pockets of his baggy trousers as he tilted his chair back up on two legs, bobbing against the wall, was a blond-haired, soft-featured man with wire glasses: Hughes. He nodded in my general direction and never spoke.

I did my bit. Molly was attentive and read with care. No one else showed much interest.

"Thanks for coming in," the casting associate muttered.

"Fuck 'em," I thought on the way out.

Once the door was shut, Molly apparently turned to John and said, "That's the kind of guy I would fall for."

"THAT wimpy guy?" John said.

"He's sensitive, poetic," Molly said.

John wasn't convinced, but over the next few days the calls to my agent went from "He did a nice job" to "We like him a lot for this." It was testament to John's belief in Molly that he got behind the idea and cast me. It was another example of what I believe was the key to John's success in his youth films. Not only on-screen did John give young people credit for being full human beings with opinions worth listening to; he carried this line of thinking through in all areas. Later, on set, John brought a small boom box around and between setups

149

would play snatches of music and ask for the actors' opinions. He was gathering information for what would become the sound track, and he wisely solicited the ears of the generation who would be listening. That sound track was as responsible for the success of the film as what appeared on the screen.

As I was offered the job only a short time before filming, and since there was no question of whether or not I would do the film, I returned to my old schoolboy ways and felt no need to read the script—until I was on the plane out to Los Angeles to begin shooting. The basic plot of the film—which John boasted he wrote in a weekend—hung on Molly's character, named Andie, wanting to go to her school prom with my character, Blane. In the end, peer pressure proves too much for Blane and he stands Andie up on the big night. Blane mopes at home and Andie takes comfort in her best friend; lesson learned. In the few scenes I had read of the script, it never occurred to me that Blane would lack moral conviction and back out. Reading on the plane, I was shocked by his spineless nature. Upon landing, I called my manager, Mary, and complained, "This guy is a total loser. I can't do this movie!"

"Honey, you read the script," Mary replied. "You knew what happened."

What could I say?

The cast had already been gathering for several days of informal rehearsals at the director Howie's home when I joined. Whereas during rehearsals for *St. Elmo's Fire* there had been an undercurrent of tension and competition, here things were loose, familial.

"Can we read the scene again?" I'd ask.

John, who would take a very active role during filming

despite his producer credit, would shrug. "We can if you want. We don't need to."

He was free and easy with changing dialogue as he heard us read, customizing it to who we were. At the end of my first day John said, "Things took a big leap today," in an offhanded way. My presence was the only thing different about rehearsal from the days before, and I silently took his comment as a vote of confidence. This indirect, almost absent fashion marked the way John would speak with me going forward. But it was enough to dispel any doubts that I might have been miscast or was there against John's instincts.

As a thank-you to Molly for getting me the part, I purchased her a large—about five feet tall—green Gumby doll, the Claymation character. Why this was how I chose to express my gratitude, I have no idea. Perhaps because it allowed me to present Molly with a card on which I had cleverly inscribed, "Gumby for you!"

Yet, as the shooting wore on—and although we are forever linked in a cinematic romance—Molly and I never grew close. I found her to be fiercely intelligent and determined. She was the epicenter of the Hughes world; no one knew it better or worked harder to maintain its integrity. Within a cast of equals, Molly was more equal, and her opinions carried added heft. So in a move that was more unconscious than deliberate, I concluded that to forge my own unique imprint—I felt my success rested on not being easily dismissed as some kind of interchangeable Hughes teen—my power on the set would come from maintaining some form of distance. That I was older than Molly—at twenty-two, I was starting to spend many of my evenings drinking in bars and clubs, while Molly was still in high school—was less responsible for the emotional gap that grew between us than this aloof position I adopted. Add to this, *St. Elmo's Fire* came out early in our shoot and my reception in it had been warm and positive. Overnight, I was a young actor on the rise. I began to be seen—and to feel—on more equal footing with the others. I started to take my space with more confidence. While my remote posture did nothing to foster a bond with Molly, the friction it created often sparked between us—and it could be argued that this tension added to an on-screen chemistry that palpably charged our scenes. But it can't be overstated that without Molly's support I never would have been cast in *Pretty in Pink*, and my career, and indeed my life, would have looked very different.

Giving Howie all he could handle on set.

Around this time my father began to call on me with growing frequency, pressing hard for more money. The bigger the job I landed, the greater his need became.

"You have my word, pal," my father always promised. "I'll pay you back every penny." His other oft-repeated assurance was, "If the situation were reversed, I'd do the same for you." And I'm sure he would have. Always, I acquiesced to my father's needs. My life was beginning to grow bigger, more public, pressing beyond the boundaries of my experience and know-how. I wasn't consciously craving support or backup, but I felt undercut and destabilized by these requests. When I tried to express these feelings to my father, he dismissed them by snapping, "Well, your feelings are wrong."

One evening early on during filming, an actor named Matthew Laurance—who had appeared in the role of Demi Moore's next-door neighbor in *St. Elmo's Fire*—dropped by the set to say hello. We went for a drink and soon became fast friends. Our haunts were not the Hollywood hot spots but the local dives—shooting pool at Barney's Beanery, throwing darts in the smoky English pubs on La Cienega Boulevard. Impulsive midnight drives to Las Vegas and high-speed races up the coast to Monterey were not uncommon. In Matthew's friendship I found a security similar to what I had enjoyed with Eddie and my brother Peter before—and at a time when I needed it most.

Up to this point, with a few exceptions, I had been largely invisible to the opposite sex. But with the recent release of *St. Elmo's Fire*, I became sprinkled with catnip.

Confidence is an attractive quality; it can carry the day over many seemingly insurmountable obstacles. And there is little that can boost the confidence of a twenty-two-year-old male like having young women find him attractive. In playing my first romantic lead, it helped that people now saw me in a romantic light for the first time—and because they suddenly did, so did I.

It became clear that my place in the sexual landscape had shifted the night that James Spader took me to the Body Shop on Sunset Boulevard to see Glitter. The Body Shop was a strip club and Glitter was, yes, a stripper. And, yes, she was dusted in select spots with glitter. Glitter was beautiful and proficient on the pole before anyone thought to use them for exercise. But what made me realize things had changed in my world was that Glitter, upon learning we were in attendance, altered her program. Whatever song she had been planning to accompany her on that pole was jettisoned for the theme song to *St. Elmo's Fire*: "Man in Motion." Her gaze was directed solely at me. Large quantities of vodka helped me to overcome my reticence, and for a short time Matthew and I became regulars in the back booth.

I took things a step further and saw Glitter outside of her work on a few occasions. On our first evening out, I drove to the Valley to pick her up at her aunt's condo off Ventura Boulevard. Glitter, whose off-stage name was Michelle, had recently moved down from Vancouver. We had dinner and a fine time at a vegetarian restaurant. The morning after our second or third get-together, I was shooting on set when the cinematographer, a gentle and nearly always silent man named Tak Fujimoto, suddenly called out, "Cut! Cut!" in the middle of a take. Everyone stopped and turned his way. "Specks on his face. Specks on his face!"

Glitter, as everyone knows, can be tricky to remove from the skin and difficult to see at certain angles, while at others it catches the light beautifully. Apparently the makeup person had missed a few specks, but the lights on set had not. Michelle and my relationship didn't go much further, but I can assure you that it had nothing to do with any further makeup mishaps. And to this story I will add only this: I have not set foot in a strip club for more than a quarter century.

—

I bought an old Camaro convertible (my first and only car) midway into filming, and one evening as I arrived at work John sauntered over.

My hot wheels.

"Hot wheels," he said, then pulled something from under his arm. "Give this a read when you have a chance." John tossed the script onto the passenger seat beside me and walked away.

We were shooting a scene at a nightclub where Jon Cryer was trying to talk his way in past the doorman, played by the comedian Andrew Dice Clay. As is often the case in film-making, I spent much of the night waiting around. I retreated to my trailer and read John's script—something called *Ferris Bueller's Day Off.* It was funny. Very. I found John on set and told him as much. He never mentioned it to me again.

But John wasn't quite done with me yet. Immediately after the film was finished, I was invited back up to the Sundance Institute, where Robert Redford once again singled me out for attention. While there, John sent me another script, called *Some Kind of Wonderful.* This time he sent it through my agent and formally asked me to do it. It struck me as virtually the same story as the one we had just completed but with the genders simply reversed. I turned it down and John and my relationship essentially ended there.

The attention that had begun to be directed at me in Los Angeles continued on the street and at my neighborhood bars in New York. I was now beginning to be seen as an object of curiosity to many. My presence was felt where it hadn't been before. My opinions seemed to have impact, and my choices began to drive encounters in a way they never had.

Aspects of selfishness and perceptions of uniqueness that are normal in children—qualities we learn to outgrow in adulthood—began to be reinforced and validated. The fledgling sense of adult identity that had been forming in me was jolted, thrown off its natural evolutionary trajectory. I began to be imbued by others with a sense of specialness, other-ness. In a typically cliché moment reminiscent of the "The

Emperor's New Clothes," I was sitting in Automatic Slim's bar on Washington Street with my old friend Seve when our table became filled with people who knew me only from the movies. Holding forth, I said something inconsequential and not particularly funny, yet the entire table burst into laughter simply because I said it. While their reaction was initially pleasing, I knew what I said wasn't funny and that the response was disproportionate. I looked across the table to my friend; his brow furrowed, then he shrugged. In that moment I got up and went home. But there were many other times when I stayed, when I would use my outsize social status to bask in similar attention, especially if it involved a pretty young woman.

I was making my first tentative steps out onto the hollow ground where fame resides. My growing profile would soon be put in front of everything else about me. A young, "hot" movie actor was who I was now, and every relationship would be altered by it.

—

When I was in college, my goal had been to have a career on the stage. It was what I was training for. My being plucked from the weeds for *Class* had altered all that. Yet a theater career was something I still wanted. And all during this time I made active efforts to pursue one.

I was a member of a small off-off-Broadway theater company called the Ensemble Studio Theatre over on West Fifty-Second Street and did plays there regularly. During the run of one such play, my father came to see the show. Outside on the sidewalk after the performance, we stood around with a few of my friends from the theater. In front of everyone, my father pulled out a wad of cash. Peeling off several bills, he insisted I take a few bucks. "Always good to have a little cash in your pocket, pal."

By this point I had been consistently giving my father large portions of my salary for several years. This gesture, in front of my friends, simultaneously embarrassed and galled me.

As this period of success began, more and more people began to ask me for money. My brother Peter, who had been my early protector, called me on the phone one afternoon. I was always happy to hear his voice and swap stories. We chatted for a while and then he mentioned that he was going to get married.

"Congratulations!" I shouted through the line.

"Yeah. So, Andy, can I borrow 7K?"

"Oh. What do you need it for?"

"To buy an engagement ring."

I suggested that this was probably not the best idea. (In the end, my brother married someone else years later.) On another occasion, when I blanched at a request for a much larger amount from another member of my family, I was reminded that "*technically* it is your money," but "it would be a nice thing to do."

I said yes more often than not—to avoid conflict, so as not to disappoint, to play big shot, or in an effort to ease someone's path, or to buy space for myself, or to try to bring us closer. But nearly every relationship in which such transactions were involved was adversely affected by it. In the end, my experience with almost every person to whom I gave money was the same: they resented me for it. Contrary to giving people a leg up, my offers were perceived as something that suggested, "I will do for you what I see you cannot do for yourself."

The money didn't feel significant or real to me in a tangible way, and so I had little invested in whether I was paid back or not, only that I felt like I was being played by those who insisted they would quickly do so and then made no efforts to that end. Finally, in an effort to remove the cloud that hung between those to whom I had loaned money and myself, and hoping to restore some balance, I simply forgave all the loans. When I did, some were grateful, others shrugged, while still others reacted with a mixture of suspicion and confusion. And until the day he died, my father continued to insist he would repay every penny. I was simply relieved to be done with it all.

The Boys of Winter was my first Broadway show. I had been advised not to do the play because of the six-month commitment it demanded. The thinking was that taking myself off the market for so long a stretch might hamper the momentum I'd begun to gather in my film career. But in my mind there was no question. If someone was offering me a job on Broadway, I was going to leap at it. Set in Vietnam, the play centered around a group of young marines on a remote mission and was written by John Pielmeier. John was the same man who wrote *Agnes of God*, the play I second-acted several times a few years earlier in order to see Amanda Plummer's performance.

The show struggled from the start. The cast included Ving Rhames, Matt Dillon, and after a few weeks Wesley Snipes took over for another actor who was let go. There were constant rewrites. New scenes were tried out in the show every evening, while other material was jettisoned, including (mercifully) the moment of my stripping naked and falling from a high tree into the waiting arms of my cast mates.

The production was directed by Herbert Ross, who had a long and successful career, first as a choreographer and later as the director of numerous works by Neil Simon. Herb was the wrong man for the job and was eventually replaced—but not before he sat us all down and singled out how each one of us had let him down.

The show was in trouble, yet the visceral response from many of those attending was palpable. Ron Kovic, a Vietnam War hero, activist, and author of the memoir *Born on the Fourth of July*, was there most evenings. Ron usually brought fellow veterans along. And after the curtain came down, we would all retire to the bar around the corner. The vets were grateful someone was trying to tell their story, while we craved their approval.

I felt expansive when I drank, in a way I wasn't when sober, my anxieties and fears subsiding. Elbows on tables cluttered with empty glasses, we all talked and cried and hugged—and drank the bar dry every night.

Then the phone rang. The studio on *Pretty in Pink* had conducted a test screening in which the audience spoke loud and clear. They'd loved the movie until my character stood Molly up at the prom. That Blane turned out to be a jerk had apparently not sat well with the audience, either. They wanted us to be together. Hughes suggested a reshoot. Paramount agreed.

But I was onstage six nights a week in New York, playing

a marine with a shaved head. I was measured for a wig. And because the show didn't end until after the last flight, Paramount sent the jet. I conjured images of an elite private plane racing me across the country, swaddled in luxury. The reality was slightly different. On the evening I was to fly, I became sick onstage and for the only time in my career left in the middle of the performance. My understudy, Rob Morrow, who would go on to television fame a few years later with *Northern Exposure*, finished the show.

In need of a wig.

As I lay on a cot backstage, I knew I wasn't truly ill. The show was faltering, I was drinking to drunkenness every evening, and the idea of a midnight flight, followed by a day of shooting in which I would need to step into true leading man shoes, followed by a quick turnaround to go before the theater critics—all within twenty-four hours—weighed on me. Stress had entered my life; I was ill-equipped to deal with it.

Since he would also be coming from New York, Jon Cryer was put on the plane as well. Jon and I had not gotten along during filming. Jon had a nervous laugh I found irritating, and my impatience with him exacerbated any feelings of insecurity he might have been experiencing, which only fed my irritation, which in turn fueled his feelings of insecurity, and around and around it went. I quietly enjoyed the power it gave me over him and justified it as perfect for the roles, and yet when Jon raged one of the film's most oft-quoted lines— "His name is Blane? That's a major appliance, not a name!"— his fury toward me was real and justified. (Decades later I ran into Jon backstage at a talk show. We laughed at our past and spoke with wonder of our shared experience and how it had followed us in a way neither of us could have ever imagined.)

Jon was accompanied by his agent. The plane was small, with only three seats and a couch. Since I was sick, I was kindly given the couch. Halfway across the country, in the middle of the night, the plane stopped to refuel in Kansas. Jon's manager complained: Why couldn't Jon get the couch for the next half of the journey? I pretended to be asleep and not to hear. A six-hour commercial flight took more than nine hours in the small plane. Perhaps Harrison Ford had been using Paramount's "A" jet.

The scenes to be reshot centered around the prom itself. Instead of skipping the event entirely, as I had in the original ending, I now appeared and approached Molly, expressed my regrets, and confessed my belief in her before whispering my love into her ear. The new ending had us kissing outside the dance in silhouette before car headlights at night—an image in perfect keeping with classic '80s MTV iconography. In reality, we shot during the day in the corner of an empty and darkened soundstage.

Audiences loved the changes and everything about the reshoot had the desired effect, including my ill-fitting and cheaply made hairpiece. It lent me a somewhat sickly appearance and enhanced my forlorn look as I approached Molly in my white tuxedo. Had the producers known we would still be talking about the movie all these years later, they might have invested in a better wig.

As the film was set for release, I was called back to Los Angeles once again for a press junket. Instead of us traveling around to promote the film, various members of the media were brought in from throughout the country for a few days of group and one-on-one interviews. It was my first experience of a media onslaught.

There was little group playfulness during the interviews. Molly was a private person, John Hughes was naturally wary of the press, and I was locked into my knee-jerk attitude of indifference in nearly all professional settings. My manager, agent, even friends had begun to mention to me that my aloof attitude gave me the appearance of not caring. Instead of looking at the causes, I simply denied that it did.

For the interviews one day, I chose to wear a pair of white painter's pants that I'd purchased in one of the secondhand shops in Greenwich Village. A bit of the hem on one of the pant legs had ripped and come down. During a group session, a reporter asked if my torn hem was a conscious fashion choice. It was at that moment that I became aware for the first time that I—like all people in my position—was being scrutinized in a way that made my position feel precarious.

The truth was that I had no idea how I might fix the hem on the pants. I couldn't sew, nor had it occurred to me to take them somewhere to have them mended. (I had never done such a thing.) I simply ignored the torn hem as a normal thing that happened to clothes.

I was taken aback by the question and felt a sudden rush of shame. I wanted to leave the room; instead, I shrugged at the reporter and mumbled, "No, I hadn't noticed it."

The reporter went on to call my look "studied casual." I liked the phrase and for a time adopted it as a self-aware way to describe my style of dress, but nothing about my look was studied, or conscious, savvy, or informed whatsoever. In regard to fashion, as was the case in so many other areas of my life, I was simply reacting to whims and transient influences, employing scant information on which to base my decisions. If I had been in any other business, I would have termed my behavior as "utterly clueless in an age-appropriate way." But in the movies, where so much money is at stake, where envy is ubiquitous and desperation drives behavior—where a hundred people line up to take your place and the whims of public sentiment and caprices of taste dictate so much—cluelessness, appropriate or not, is a frailty one cannot afford.

Add to this something I did not yet understand. If you are out beyond the safety of the herd, exposed and alone on the leading edge, you are fair game. I say this without complaint or even an opinion. It is simply the way that it is, and something of which I was not aware. Nothing illustrates this point more than a cover story that appeared on the June 10, 1985, edition of *New York* magazine called "Hollywood's Brat Pack."

The photo splashed across the front of the magazine was a publicity shot from *St. Elmo's Fire* of Emilio Estevez, Judd Nelson, and Rob Lowe. I recognized the image because I was originally in it, but for the purposes of the article I had been trimmed out. The story, by a writer named David Blum, was intended to be a small feature on Emilio in advance of the release of the movie. What it became was a stinging indictment of a group of young, successful actors. Emilio had made a naïve error in judgment—which was odd when you consider that he grew up in a showbiz family as the son of Martin Sheen, and should have known to be more media conscious. He had invited the writer along with him on an evening at the Hard Rock Cafe with some of his buddies, who happened to be Judd and Rob. It was a planned gathering for the press, and it backfired. The three ran into a few other actors, behaved stupidly—as young men who are drinking are apt to do—acting with entitlement, trash-talking other actors, and recklessly flirting with young women. While perhaps not a world away from their typical behavior, the fact that it was a staged event lent the evening a falseness that omitted the actors' charms, complexity, and humanity. And from this artificially concocted evening, the Brat Pack was born.

Ronald Reagan's Great Right Hope, by Lally Weymouth
Fashion: Easy, Breezy—and Priced-Right—Summer Style

NEW YORK

HOLLYWOOD'S BRAT PACK

BY DAVID BLUM

Rob Lowe, Judd Nelson, and Emilio Estevez in the forthcoming *St. Elmo's Fire.*

And it began...

I was back in New York and not present on the night in question. Nor does it appear likely that I would have been invited along had I been in LA. My name appeared just once, late in the article:

166

And of Andrew McCarthy, one of the New York–based actors in *St. Elmo's Fire*, a costar says, "He plays all his roles with too much of the same intensity, I don't think he'll make it." The Brat Packers save their praise for themselves.

The fallout from the article was immediate and charged. High-powered publicists—the same ones who had arranged the interview and the evening out—struggled, with no success, for damage control. The phrase entered the zeitgeist, and the branding instantly burned deeper than anyone could have predicted.

Having been excluded from the group of actors cited in the story as the leading crop of up-and-comers making their mark in the current slate of successful youth films, I simply felt hurt that one of the three guys had said such a dismissive thing about me. This Brat Pack stuff was not my problem. In fact, I concluded, they brought it on themselves with their arrogant, callous behavior. Good luck to them.

Now who was being naïve?

Riding It

AT 11:00 P.M. on February 27, 1986, I was shivering, standing on the curb beside the newsstand outside the Christopher Street subway station at Sheridan Square, waiting for the *New York Times* to be dropped out of the back of a truck. I had never waited for a review before. While I hadn't felt as emotionally invested in *Pretty in Pink* as I had in *St. Elmo's Fire*, on a purely business level I had begun to wake up. I knew that how this movie was received mattered greatly to my future.

The review in the paper was begrudgingly positive. I was surprised. I had thought the story about a girl and boy from opposite sides of the tracks was skin-deep, and the big finale about going to a dance pretty insignificant. Add to this that by now I was becoming used to the films I was in garnering fairly dismissive reviews, I was expecting the worst. Pauline Kael in the *New Yorker* didn't disappoint, describing the movie as "slight and vapid...with the consistency of watery jello." The *Washington Post* said it was "as fraudulent as the junk it's supposed to transcend." And the *Chicago Tribune* dismissed the

168

film as "much like the worst in American television." Others were less harsh, although not much.

But kids don't read reviews. They went. They related. And I became famous among my generation.

I was successful in *Pretty in Pink* for the exact reason that Molly had surmised I would be—which was also the reason that I was almost not cast. Although I had been the third-string quarterback on my peewee league football team when I was twelve, there was little chance anyone was going to confuse me with the football stud originally intended in the script. But I had an emotional availability that was difficult to mask. I also had another thing going for me. In this movie, as in *St. Elmo's Fire*, I radiated a freshness, a sense of discovery, that can be captured only in passing. It's a moment of youth that transcends talent or acting ability. It is a quality, not a skill.

Earning my heartthrob credentials.

I boast no comparison when I say it's a quality that James Dean displayed in *East of Eden*; Emily Watson had it in *Breaking the Waves*; and it was undeniable in Leonardo DiCaprio in *What's Eating Gilbert Grape*. There are countless other examples. Like the first light of dawn, there is a transitory magic in it, a singular quality, something so fresh it seems it must be occurring for the first time. It's something we as an audience get to piggyback on and relive or discover in ourselves vicariously. Over this, a deep bond between actor and audience can be created. Only after this moment—which seems it can never end even as it's vanishing—does the long day develop and careers are made or not.

As the years have gone by, there are clips from these early movies that invariably surface again and again. And while I can occasionally shudder at my acting, there is no denying the simple joy at being there, at being alive and young and discovering who I am, all captured on-screen in real time.

I knew that I was now famous because things that happen to famous people began to happen to me. Strangers gave me things I didn't need, others wanted to have sex with me, and other (more) famous people began to reach out to me. I got a call that Warren Beatty wanted to meet with me: "Be at the bar of the Polo club on Fifty-Seventh at 7:00 p.m. tonight. Warren wants to talk to you about a project." We met and the legend obliquely expressed interest in me for a movie, but all I could concentrate on was the bowl of peanuts on the bar in front of us that he devoured, rakishly popping them into his mouth one after another in movie icon fashion. I never heard from him again.

One day I received a call out of the blue from someone in Andy Warhol's world asking if I would like to join Andy and some friends for dinner. I quickly said yes, but as the day wore on, my anxiety over the dinner grew. Not long before the appointed time, I called back and concocted a ludicrous story that my cat had jumped out the window and I had to go and find her; perhaps another time. The woman on the other end of the phone made no pretense of believing me. For years I regretted my timidity, until fairly recently, when I mentioned the incident to my wife as we walked through a Warhol exhibit in a museum. I expected her to scold me for yet another display of my reticence, when she surprised me (as usual) and said, "You probably just didn't want to be treated as an amusement."

On another occasion I received a shirt from Tommy Hilfiger in the mail. How the hell did Tommy get my address on West Twelfth Street? Included was a note saying that Tommy loved my work and would like me to have some of his. It was several sizes too large for me, but I wore it out nonetheless. In LA, I participated in a 1980s Hollywood rite of passage by attending a party at the Playboy Mansion. Beautiful young women mingled while James Caan and a few older comedians smoked cigars. I watched "Hef" descend the grand staircase smoking his pipe, wearing red silk pajamas, a blonde on each elbow. I wandered out of the Tudor Revival villa and stumbled into a peacock. Inside the pool grotto I interrupted a frolicking couple; they didn't care.

There were other, less playful examples that my place in the world had changed. I had lost active contact with most of my college classmates, but one evening I went out with a few old acquaintances from school. We ended up back at my apartment for a drink. I was still living in the small one-bedroom with the sloping floors and the faulty fireplace. We were chatting away, when suddenly one of the guys leaned forward and spat on my floor. I was taken aback.

"Clean that up," I said.

"What are you going to do about it?"

I had known all evening that beneath my former schoolmate's "Good for you" platitudes resided this resentment that epitomized his true feeling. While my wary, even suspicious nature was no doubt responsible for blocking out opportunities for friendship and intimacy, there was no denying that I also possessed a vigilant third eye that was perceptive in the ways of falsehood. During this phase and beyond, I used experiences such as my classmate's floor spitting as proof of people's insincerity. I used it to further isolate myself—to my own detriment.

It was around this time that strangers also began to approach me and say, "I met your father." They would describe how he had stopped them on a street corner, or interrupted them at the next table in a restaurant. My dad had gotten into the habit of asking unsuspecting people if they knew who Andrew McCarthy was. And if they did, he launched in. I would apologize to his victims profusely and slink away, humiliated and mortified. When I pleaded with my father to stop this behavior, he dismissed my complaints with a wave of his hand. It took years for me to lose the anger and shame with which I viewed these encounters and finally see them with affection.

After the success of *Pretty in Pink*, I was suddenly offered work for the first time. That I was now asked to do what I had to scramble for in the not-so-distant past was something I simply experienced as a relief. I didn't shift my thinking or begin strategizing. I didn't pause to ask where I wanted to be in five years, let alone ten or twenty.

I look with admiration at young actors who break out and then begin to acquire intellectual properties, option material, and create projects for themselves. Perhaps it was simply my lack of vision, but I continued looking only for the next crumb that was dropped in front of me. And what came next was a movie called *Mannequin*.

I read the script and accepted the offer. Then, shortly before filming, I read it again. "What was I thinking?" I asked myself. Had I simply been blinded by someone wanting to give me a job?

Inspired by the vintage film *One Touch of Venus*, our movie centered on a young department store window dresser who falls in love with a mannequin that comes to life only for him. It's unlikely that such a movie would be made today. What is even more unlikely is that it was a big hit—and is still beloved by a certain subset of people today. If I'm to speak the truth, I hold the movie in a special place of affection as well. There was an innocence about it, and an open heart. It was playful in a time of all-knowing '80s cynicism, written and directed by a similarly childlike man named Michael Gottlieb. Michael was an avid motorcycle rider, and it was his idea that I ride a Harley-Davidson in the film. I hated that fucking bike and dreaded every scene I had on it. (Years later Michael was killed riding one of his beloved motorcycles along a winding mountain road. When I saw his daughter sometime after, we agreed that at least it was as Michael would like to have gone.)

For the first time, I owned my space as the lead character and took stage when it needed to be taken; I was simply and finally ready. During one scene I was summoned to the board-room and, instead of being fired, was given a promotion. As everyone walked out, in one swift move I impulsively leapt into a chair with my feet landing up on the table, crossed at the ankles. After Michael called cut, the producer came rushing over to me and said, "Do more of that kind of stuff."

Between takes I would huddle in a corner of the set, swilling Coke and listening to Bob Seger's song "Feel Like a Number" over and over again on my new Walkman. When I wasn't

Making Mannequin *and being the center of attention.*

doing that, I was flirting with the still photographer. All the while, I was very aware that I was the center of attention as I had never been before and that the weight of the film's success or failure rested on me. I welcomed the responsibility. I was by now entirely comfortable on a film set, I understood the structure, and I felt safer there than anywhere else. I worked with confident relish.

We filmed almost entirely at night, after closing time in Wanamaker's department store in Philadelphia. It was a vampire existence of up all night and sleep all day. Upon completion of shooting each dawn, much of the crew, including myself, was in the habit of returning to the production office in the hotel where we were all staying, then drinking for several hours before heading to bed for the day. I was drinking to excess on a near-daily basis. Yet I still experienced it as a point of pride. I took from it a feeling of power. I was an adult, a man—in a long line of successful cinematic drinkers. I viewed little about my drinking with alarm or regret, even as there were days when it caused me trouble and compromised my work.

In a silly sequence, an homage to the silent films of Harold Lloyd, my character, Jonathan, got tangled up on a sign outside the store that began to swing wildly back and forth high above the ground while I got electric shocks from a cable. I chose the wrong day to have a vicious hangover and suffered every take of that swinging sign with vows to not drink again anytime soon. But after wrap that day I was back in the production office downing beers.

Originally titled *Perfect Timing*, the name was changed in postproduction. What idiots the publicity people are, I thought. I had a similar reaction years later when I learned that

Regretting those extra beers now.

a new broadcast platform called Netflix was going to release all episodes of a show I had directed called *Orange Is the New Black* in one day. "Every episode on the same day!" I scoffed to the producer at the time. "That's the stupidest idea I ever heard." It's wise I have never tried to make my living in promotion.

The last scene shot during filming was one of the final moments in the movie. Another character dove into a large pile of junk on a conveyor belt in hopes of discovering within it his own living mannequin. (I did mention the movie was ridiculous.) I stood off to the side and watched the scene being filmed. I vividly recall feeling very still inside—not the usual relieved high that accompanied the final day on other shoots. I didn't have a feeling of pride so much as one of simple knowing. When the movie proved a surprise hit, I was less surprised than most.

In March of 1987, I got a call. Would I like to fly to Los Angeles and participate in Paramount Pictures' Seventy-Fifth Anniversary celebration? It would entail a gathering on a soundstage for a few hours of mingling, and the main event would be a group shot of movie stars in front of the Paramount gate. I was awed, excited, and intimidated. Paramount had produced *Pretty in Pink* a year earlier, and as *Mannequin* had just been released to surprisingly large numbers, the notion that I was a star on the rise must have been the reason for my last-minute invitation. Nothing was being asked of me other than that I enjoy my time among Hollywood legends, yet my anxiety about the event grew as I flew west the day before the gathering. I checked into the Sunset Marquis hotel and ordered a few drinks—so many drinks that I was making such a racket that hotel security had to knock on my door and ask me to keep it down. It was the only time security has ever been called on me in a hotel—and I was alone. What had I been doing? The next morning I was suffering so badly with anxiety and one of the worst hangovers of my life that I asked the driver to circle the studio a few times before I could get up the nerve to go in.

I mostly cowered in a corner of the soundstage as the stars mingled. I chatted briefly with the president of Paramount, Ned Tanen, and Tom Cruise, whom I'd met lightly a few times before. Tom owned the conversation in his bold red sweater, and I slunk away wondering how he could be so confident in a room full of Hollywood royalty. One of the many publicists on hand to facilitate the day kept approaching me and asking

My hometown theater. I was thrilled to receive this photo in the
mail anonymously.

if there was anyone I would like to meet: Elizabeth Taylor?
Gregory Peck? Burt Lancaster?

"I'd like to meet Jimmy Stewart," I finally confessed. I had
first encountered the legend just over half a decade earlier, in
the dark of the 8th Street Playhouse, watching him flirt with
Katharine Hepburn in *Philadelphia Story*. As I made my way
across the soundstage, that felt like a lifetime ago.

James Stewart extended his hand and stammered the way
only Jimmy Stewart could stammer, "Pl-pl-pleasure to meet
you, young man." I felt as if he looked through me with a
knowing and slightly sad disapproval, but I knew even then
that it was simply a projection of my own feelings about my
hungover, shame-filled condition.

At one point I was asked to join a photo that was being assembled with Harrison Ford, Robert De Niro, Debra Winger, Faye Dunaway, Tom Cruise, and Molly Ringwald (whom I never even spoke to on this day). I demurred, and Tim Hutton filled the final spot. That photo appeared on the cover of *Life* magazine the next month.

I've grown to forgive many of the internal conflicts within my nature, as well as my drinking past, but occasional and blatant flashes of self-sabotage such as this are still difficult to reconcile.

As the day wore on, my sense of self-imprisonment, of self-flagellation, grew worse. I remained paralyzed off to the side as the others mingled. Then, as everyone was being gathered up to go outside, Henry Winkler, whom I had grown up watching as Fonzie on *Happy Days*, rescued me. He led me to bleachers in front of the iconic Paramount gates. Henry kept me close and pulled me into position. And there I am in the photo, occupying my familiar spot on the edge of things, clinging to the third row, next to Henry, behind Olivia de Havilland, in front of William Shatner.

All during this period, it was strongly suggested to me—by agents, my manager, business acquaintances, as well as friends—that I should move west. Even more than today, the epicenter of the movie industry was in Los Angeles. If you were in the business, the wisdom went, you should be around town, go to a few parties, attend a premiere or two, show your face. It was an industry built on relationships, and they would carry you further than talent. Yet I continued to struggle with

From left to right, front row: *Martha Raye, Dana Andrews, Elizabeth Taylor, Frances Dee, Joel McCrea, Harry Dean Stanton, Harrison Ford, Jennifer Beals, Marlee Matlin, Danny DeVito.* Second row: *Olivia de Havilland, Kevin Costner, Cornel Wilde, Don Ameche, DeForest Kelley, Tom Cruise, Charlton Heston, Penny Marshall, Bob Hope, Victor Mature, Elizabeth McGovern, Robert De Niro.* Third row: *Andrew McCarthy, Henry Winkler, Anthony Perkins, Robert Stack, Mark Harmon, Faye Dunaway, Buddy Rogers, Gregory Peck, Debra Winger, Timothy Hutton.* Fourth row: *Jane Russell, Mike Connors, John Travolta, Janet Leigh, Charles Bronson, Ted Danson, Louis Gossett Jr., Ryan O'Neal, Rhonda Fleming, Leonard Nimoy.* Fifth row: *William Shatner, Peter Graves, Molly Ringwald, Dorothy Lamour, Olivia Newton-John, Cindy Williams, Matthew Broderick, Gene Hackman, Walter Matthau, Robin Williams.* Back row: *Ali MacGraw, Burt Lancaster, Scott Baio, Rhea Perlman, Bruce Dern, James Caan, Glenn Ford, Fred MacMurray, Shelley Long, James Stewart.*

what felt to me like solely transactional business encounters. They felt transparent, false; I was too embarrassed to hustle for myself. Because every relationship I had in Los Angeles was associated with show business, and every place I went carried a show business connection—since the sole reason for my being there was to get work or carry out work—I felt like a phony whenever I hung around to see or be seen. And since everyone I knew was associated with work, I was often comparing myself to others. I found driving down Sunset Boulevard a petri dish for my resentments and jealousies. More than once I looked up to see a billboard for a new film I wasn't in and muttered to myself in the car, "I never even heard about that movie."

I couldn't even comfortably walk the streets as I did in New York. Whenever I went for a stroll on the broad avenues of Los Angeles, I felt exposed and vulnerable on the deserted streets. With nowhere I could really land, I rarely relaxed.

Yet I wasn't so jaded—even in my early twenties—to believe that all relationships in Hollywood were a means to an end. I understood that true connections between people who shared so much must be commonplace. I simply came down in the place of feeling on the outside—although there were occasional moments of genuine contact. The first Hollywood party I ever attended was at Marty Ransohoff's home. Marty had been the producer of *Class*, my first film, and shortly before its release he threw an old-fashioned Hollywood bash. I ended up sitting at the knee of James Coburn. Tall, rake thin, his craggy hands crippled by arthritis, he puffed steadily on a fat cigar and told me how friendship in Hollywood was essential if you were to survive it. With the same authority he displayed on-screen, he was generous with me, gentle, and wise. I never saw him again, but ever since I've quietly considered James Coburn my Hollywood god-father. Whenever I see him on-screen, I feel my shoulders drop.

Back in New York, when I wasn't working, I could go about my mundane routines that had little to do with the weekly grosses or reading *Variety*. And very few of my friends were in show business—which doesn't mean they weren't business-savvy people. My friend Seve was a highly successful salesman for the dental industry and operated in a world far removed from show business. And although these were the days long before terms like "brand" were freely applied to human beings, a favorite topic of Seve's—once a few drinks had been consumed—was how I needed to approach myself in my career as if I were a commodity. To think in this way reminded me of how my father conducted business, with every relationship and encounter geared toward a specific goal. Yet I knew that Seve, as well as those folks out in Hollywood, were correct. I simply didn't have the wherewithal to navigate myself as if I were a business. In defensive arrogance, I scoffed at my friend, claiming his approach was a kind of artistic blasphemy. What I wasn't then, and never became, was a businessman.

I was at a pivotal point in my career and my life. I got away with *Mannequin* simply because it made money, but it was not the type of film a serious career was built upon; Martin Scorsese or Steven Spielberg were not likely to call me up based on my work in a dance montage with a live dummy in a department store. I spoke of wanting more serious opportunities, but silently questioned my belief that I could work with such masters. I made few serious efforts to that end.

And the Brat Pack label didn't help. Because it was such a well-turned phrase, it had quickly spread to include young and successful actors beyond the initial group from the article. And because I had appeared right alongside Emilio, Judd, and Rob in *St. Elmo's Fire*, and then when *Pretty in Pink* instantly proved seminal to that same youth generation, I was swallowed up into the heart of it. No matter that I had been disparaged by the original Brats. I became a card-carrying charter member.

The irony, of course, was that even as the Brat Pack was becoming solidified in the mind of the public, each successive mention in the press helped to ensure its dissolution. Immediately after the article appeared, actors began to actively avoid making any movie that might be considered a Brat Pack endeavor, and helped to kill off the current cycle of youth ensemble movies. An every-man-for-himself attitude pervaded as actors ran for whatever cover they could find or invent.

In a gesture as effective as sticking my finger into the crack of a crumbling levee, I took the stance of shrugging off the whole Brat Pack mess and saying it would pass. Yet the ferocity with which the term was flung about only grew in intensity. So when I was asked to go to France to do a small part in an independent film called *Waiting for the Moon*, I did so because I had never been to Europe, not because I thought it might help to distance me from the Brat Pack. (It didn't.)

Half a dozen years earlier—in adolescent naïveté and innocence—I had quietly pitched myself toward an improbable path and it had brought me here. Now a longer view was needed, and my freelancer mentality wasn't suited for distant gazing. With the wisdom of hindsight, it's easy to see that the smart move might have been to stop and let the dust settle, or go back and do more plays, or simply disappear for a time— any number of things instead of what I did do.

I rushed forward, doing three movies over the next year and drinking hard. Fear that all this might vanish was no doubt a part of the reason for the hard push, but when *Less Than Zero* came up, it seemed like the kind of serious movie I'd been aching to be a part of and it was easy to justify going after. Bret Easton Ellis's debut novel had become a sensation. Centered on the dissolute lives of a group of swaddled Beverly Hills youths, it was being made into a film by 20th Century Fox. The director, an Englishman named Marek Kanievska, didn't picture me in the role of Clay, the narrator who returns to his privileged life after a semester at an East Coast college only to see things with disillusioned eyes. But because of my current level of success, I was favored by the studio for the role. For the first and only time in my career, I did a proper screen test, with a 35mm camera and full lighting. I was tense and careful in my audition with Jami Gertz but was rammed through by the executives and awarded the part.

We never did any proper rehearsing, but while still in pre-production I spent an evening out in West Hollywood with Robert Downey Jr. In a simplistic and misguided effort to cultivate the dynamic that existed between our characters, the director had secretly issued instructions to Bobby to "get into as much trouble as you can. Have Andrew get you out of it." Marek had shared nothing about this with me. Bobby, whom I found to be sweet and authentic in our few previous encounters, seemed forced in his behavior and attitude that night. He jumped out into traffic on Melrose Avenue and I lunged after him. I apologized to strangers he harassed on the street, and tried in vain to prevent him from intruding on diners at outdoor tables. As Bobby had a history of drug use, a young man had been assigned to accompany him for the duration of filming in order to keep him on the straight and narrow. He did nothing to alter Bobby's behavior on this night. (He was also in on the ruse.) Exasperated, I finally shouted at Bobby as he ran off after a group of young women, "What the fuck are you doing?"

At which point I was filled in on Marek's instructions. I left Bobby to his minder and went home.

The script we were presented with at the beginning of shooting, by a writer named Harley Peyton, bore no resemblance to the original screenplay I had agreed to do, one written by the playwright Michael Cristofer. Not a line from the book remained.

A year of reaping rewards and easy pleasure was about to come to a grinding halt. The filming was tense and largely joyless. As a middle-class East Coast kid, I felt miscast as a Beverly Hills boy of means; the feeling that I was somehow an impostor in the role was a sensation I never shook. And I knew the director felt the same way. The *New York Times* review later took note when it graciously pointed out that my performance "showed some strain." The filmmakers went to great pains with the spectacular physical look, which only exacerbated a developing problem. I was growing increasingly self-conscious about how I looked on-screen: From which angles did I look best, which were less flattering? While my growing technical curiosity was helpful on one hand, a constant internal eye on how I appeared was something I found increasingly difficult to shake. This utterly self-defeating vanity wasn't aided on the day Marek insisted to the director of photography—a gifted geek named Ed Lachman—that he alter a shot. "I'm not going to shoot his face from an angle it can't take," Marek spat at Ed as I sat a few feet away in front of the lens.

Others were clearly struggling as well. Bobby—who turned in a haunting performance and years later would go on to become everyone's favorite superhero—was deep into his well-documented self-immolation, while Marek was beleaguered by the studio. The executives quickly realized we were making a movie about kids similar to their own privileged Beverly Hills children and that the film did not present them in a flattering light. Jami Gertz, a well-meaning and gentle soul, seemed as lost as I felt.

Smiling drug dealers regularly popped by the set like FedEx deliverymen. One of the hairdressers nodded off from misjudging his morning heroin intake and burned one of the actresses with a curling iron. And while I had tried it before, for the first time I attempted to act while on cocaine. If tension is the enemy of good acting, what part of doing cocaine—which does nothing but create tension—could be considered a good idea? Tension aside, I almost gave myself a heart attack one evening. The scene required me to dive into a pool and swim toward an underwater camera. We were filming in the LA winter, but the pool was unheated. Before the shot I took a hit of cocaine, and as I dove into the freezing water, my chest constricted in a way I hope to never feel again.

I felt under strain during the entire shoot—a feeling enhanced no doubt by my alcohol (and drug) intake—and for the first time I dreaded going to work.

Late in the filming we relocated to Palm Springs for the

climax of the movie. The mood on the shoot turned from dark to nefarious. Night shooting twisted internal rhythms, strange hangers-on proffered drugs, a sexual encounter with someone working behind the scenes on the film soured a previously pleasant relationship, and the portions of the script to be shot were themselves full of self-hate and degradation, culminating with the death of Bobby's character in the desert at dawn as the camera in a helicopter swooped in and shredded the morning. I didn't go back to Palm Springs for twenty years.

The film, already a bastardized version of the book, was further watered down when the studio insisted on reshoots. This was the era of Nancy Reagan's "Just Say No" antidrug campaign, and scenes of flushing cocaine down the drain were added. Where the director Marek wanted to make a movie that observed this subculture without judgment, the studio needed a message. The film looked beautiful and had a terrific sound track but was a hapless hybrid and unsuccessful. And for the first time I felt I had really failed: my performance was unfocused and weak.

It didn't help that the night before filming on *Less Than Zero* began, I was standing on the balcony of my room at the Chateau Marmont, staring out, when my phone rang. Since my first stay there five years earlier when I was flown in to meet Jacqueline Bisset, I had always found the hotel lonely and slightly sinister around the edges. Why I chose to stay there again after abandoning it perhaps speaks to my state of mind as filming began.

My father was on the line. By now I knew what he wanted and wasn't surprised when he pressed me for money. I found his timing, on the eve of a movie paycheck coming my way,

Most days on the set of Less Than Zero *felt about like this.*

too convenient. He continued to insist that he would pay me back in no time. This pretense, on top of his ever-increasing desperation, had created a constant strain between us, and we almost never spoke unless he needed money. I had certainly stopped calling him. I felt I was being played, just as he might con one of his clients. I wanted to help, I felt obliged to help, and I had ambivalence about the money that was being directed at me—but as I stared at the Marlboro Man billboard that stood just out the window of my room, my father told me he would jump off a roof if he didn't get more of my money. I told him to jump.

I was not the only one being affected by my dad's growing instability. Around this time my mother took my younger brother and left my father after nearly thirty years of marriage. She found a small carriage house, got herself a job, and set up a life for herself and Justin, still a teenager. My father became erratic and intrusive. Restraining orders were issued. Eventually he gave up the fight and didn't show up in court. The fact that I learned most of the details of this only after the fact—that I was privy to little of my parents' dissolving marriage and heartache—shows how wholly consumed in my own life I had become.

With Matt Dillon in Kansas—*and doing my best Montgomery Clift imitation.*

Once *Less Than Zero* was behind me, I quickly went to work on a movie called *Kansas*, about two drifters who meet on a freight train and end up robbing a bank. It was an old-style, almost dated movie, simplistic in its story line, and one I probably shouldn't have done. It was being produced by a second-rate company. But I'd signed on before I got *Less Than Zero* and I liked the idea of having a few jobs lined up, something I never had in the past.

We shot in Lawrence, Kansas, home to the University of Kansas. Once word got out that the Hollywood circus was in town, the basement bar in the hotel grew more and more crowded and filming got less and less of my attention. It felt like the college fraternity experience I never had.

While in Kansas, I purchased my mother a new car for her birthday. It was a sporty little convertible, one she'd mentioned admiringly. Since I was stuck in the heartland, I asked my brother Peter to deliver it to her. He obliged but seemed strangely hesitant about it. Although we have never discussed it, my sudden and surprising success must have been strange for my older siblings. To have their little brother become famous out of the blue when they were just in their mid- and late twenties and still trying to find their own place in the world—it could not have been easy. While success lubricated most interactions, there was nothing about my very rapid and public achievements that soothed my family life. Instead of leaning on my family for guidance through this unknown territory, I pulled further away.

Little about *Kansas* is memorable, but even so, after the strain and pressure of *Less Than Zero*, it felt like a simpler, less high-stakes time. (When my mother saw the film—one of at least a dozen people to do so—she rightly remarked on my vague and overly restrained performance: "I think you've seen one too many Montgomery Clift films, dear.")

Soon after the shoot, I found myself back in Los Angeles, hanging around, drinking, taking a few meetings, killing time. I had enjoyed the heartland so much, I convinced my friends Seve and Brian, a raspy-voiced character actor I had met during my ill-fated Broadway turn in *The Boys of Winter*, who both happened to be in LA at the time, to get a car and drive home across the country with me. Fueled by not insignificant amounts of cocaine, we rented a Volvo (for safety) and headed east. We made it past Las Vegas without incident, but I almost got in a fistfight in a bar in Colorado Springs. I had not gotten in a fight since fourth grade, when the other smallest kid in the class and I used to routinely scrape. Since we were the two tiniest ones, we wisely knew we could not do each other much damage. But the guy in the bar in Colorado Springs wasn't tiny at all and he didn't like the way I made his girlfriend laugh, and we had to move fast.

We stopped in Lawrence, Kansas, but the party was long over. After my stories of all the good times, my friends looked at me with suspicion as we ordered drinks in the deserted and depressing hotel basement bar. But while there I got a call. There was a movie happening, starring my partner from *Pretty in Pink*, Molly Ringwald, and directed by a man named David Anspaugh, who had recently directed a rousing movie called *Hoosiers*. They were both in Kentucky, scouting locations, and would meet with me if I could get there the next day. Seve, Brian, and I had renewed focus now and powered east through the night. In the middle of Missouri, flashing red lights behind pulled us over. In the backseat I had a small mound of cocaine spread out, and as Seve hit the brakes it flew everywhere. I quickly began to sniff up as much as I could as the policeman made his way to our car. Seve rolled down the window. The hot night air rushed in.

"I must have gotten caught on that downslope back there, Officer," Seve said.

The plains were flat to the horizon. The cop flashed his light through the car, into the backseat, and across my face. I tried to look as if I had just woken up instead of as if my heart were about to explode out of my chest. The car interior looked like what it was, filthy from three idiots who had been essentially living in it for two weeks as they blundered across the country.

"Slow down," the highway patrolman said, and walked away.

I met Molly and David in a hotel that was modeled after a medieval castle alongside the highway in Alexandria, Kentucky. We talked through the movie, about a rich guy who meets a backwoods Kentucky girl and a rocky romance ensues. It was based on an off-Broadway play called *Fresh Horses*, and it was a bad idea from the start. Since I continued to operate from my freelancer mentality of "Just get the next job," I spent our meeting convincing the two that capitalizing on Molly's and my recent successful partnership would be a good idea. Molly was somewhat leery after my distant behavior during *Pretty in Pink* and wisely had reservations. But I was convincing. By the end of our afternoon together we were all of a mind that the history Molly and I shared was nothing but an asset and would help parlay this effort to success.

I was wrong. Molly was miscast, and my attention was more on the hotel bar, where I would drink to inebriation every evening and get up to dance solo on the empty dance floor to Bruce Springsteen's "Pink Cadillac." The movie was a misfire. The striving that had accompanied my first several films had been replaced by a kind of inner evasion fueled by the drink, which had now become a thing unto itself.

Over the course of a few years, alcohol had gone from an adolescent amusement, a diversion representing an under-examined idea of manhood, an imitation of my cinematic heroes, to—and seemingly all of a sudden—the dominant force in my life, influencing all of my actions.

If, as is generally accepted, one's identity is obfuscated when one crosses the line into alcohol abuse, it follows that it must also cloud acting—which should be nothing if not clear-eyed access to the self. Increasingly, I felt as if I existed behind a layer of opaque plexiglass through which I viewed the world and which would clear only when I took a drink (but which of course only clouded again once I sobered up). Excessive drinking is blamed on many things: societal pressures, family issues, work stresses, anxieties, doubts and fears. And while I used alcohol as a temporary panacea for these ills and more, I knew they were not at the root of my drinking problem. I was dimly aware, even then, that my alcoholism was a primary affliction in and of itself, not a reaction to anything else.

While many of my cinematic heroes have glorified alcohol's charms and devils, I have come to understand alcoholism as something that lacks any real drama. Endless rationalizations and explanations—using alcohol to unlock creativity, calling it a tonic for the "tortured artist," and even simply labeling it "a good man's failing"—are all fallacies adopted for sensational and self-glorifying reasons to theatricalize and justify the mundane, singular, and selfish tragedy that excessive drinking creates. A phrase I heard years after I stopped drinking sums up alcohol abuse more simply and accurately than anything else I've heard: "The man takes a drink, then the drink takes a drink, then the drink takes the man." Instead of doubling my efforts to raise my acting game when my career needed it most, I had detoured and was on my way to being "taken."

But my early interest in the camera and the technical aspects of filmmaking became my lifeline. Since I was agile and quick on the uptake, I presented a strong degree of professional competence and flexibility on set. Few actors with my level of experience were more aware of filmmaking's needs. Add to this—perhaps in reaction to my early belief that I lacked a strong work ethic—that I was never late to work or unprepared when I arrived. The job I was doing mattered a great deal to me; nothing was more important. That I was often bewildered by my own drinking behavior didn't change this. I valued my position deeply. Success, in many ways, made me feel whole: It instilled in me a sense of internal power I had always craved. And it had given me an identity in the world: movie star.

I hadn't gone into acting to find fame, but fame of a certain variety had found me. Yet, while I was growing accustomed to the corner softening and indulgencies it offered, I was simultaneously aware of the self-consuming nature of fame. I began to see fame—which has no intrinsic value of its own— as an uninteresting goal. I knew I didn't have the stamina and pure hunger to pitch myself purely in its direction. But even armed with this growing knowledge, a voice inside me still whispered, "Who would I be without fame's identity-glossing patina?"

Instead of allowing success to open up a world of opportunity for me, I began to view it increasingly from the other end of the telescope.

⟵

And in a curious twist of timing—because of the lag between filming and release—I continued to grow more popular even as my work became more distracted and unfocused.

All three films I made in 1987 were failures, both creatively and commercially.

Luckily, a dead man saved me.

Surviving It

I WAS ASKED to play the nice guy—the one who gets the girl—in a hilarious, incredibly stupid (high compliment) black comedy about a pair of hapless low-level employees who are invited out to their boss's Hampton beach house for the weekend, only to discover on arrival that Bernie, their boss, is dead. Whereupon the two knuckleheads decide to not waste their few days by the sea and conclude to simply pretend that Bernie is alive. Mayhem ensues. I loved the script for *Hot and Cold*—later and wisely retitled *Weekend at Bernie's*—but instead of playing the earnest Richard, I was interested in the ne'er-do-well, harebrained Larry. Ted Kotcheff, the director, agreed.

But I needed to address something else first. Most of my drinking had been done away from the limelight, in quiet neighborhood bars. I was not a public "party boy"; I did little that was sensational, apart from occupy a corner barstool. However, people in my life had begun to take note of my drinking.

I had tried going back to my teacher Terry's Saturday morning class, and one day after a session she pulled me aside. She had heard that I was perhaps drinking too much: Was this true? Of course not, I assured her, and my attendance faded away entirely. On *Fresh Horses,* a friend of the director who had come to visit was more direct, saying, "Wow, you really drink." And there were others. I decided to stop.

I knew that the previous year had been an indulgent one personally and a lost one professionally. I needed to get back on track. A few months before *Bernie* was scheduled to begin, I put down the drink. Never a home drinker, I stopped going out. If one does not require medical withdrawal from alcohol, a supreme act of will can sometimes be enough to stop...at least for a while.

Shortly before the start of filming on *Bernie,* I checked my answering machine to find that I'd received a call from Robert Redford's office. I had been asked to do a film on which he was one of the producers. It was something I'd workshopped at his Sundance Institute, and I of course wanted to be a part of anything Redford was associated with, but I was hesitant to commit. My character had to run around stark naked through the first several minutes of the film, and I simply couldn't imagine myself doing it. Just hours before Redford's call, I had looked myself up and down in the mirror one last time and finally told my agent that I'd be passing on the project.

I called Redford back, twice, but he must have already heard the news. Had we connected directly, I'm certain I would have acquiesced to his wishes regardless of my insecurities. I was never invited back to Sundance—although I left the message from Redford's office on my answering machine for some time.

We began shooting on *Bernie* during a heat wave in August in New York City.

Affectionately basing my character on my old friend Eddie, right down to the smoking of Lucky Strikes, I felt at home in my purple high-tops from the start. Ted was supportive. After an early rehearsal he commented, "I like this guy you're creating. He's a lovable jerk." It was only my second time filming in New York, and the first on the streets of Manhattan, further enhancing my feeling of familiarity. This, on top of my head being clear from lack of drink, and I felt like myself again.

After a few weeks we shifted filming to the North Carolina coast, standing in for the Hamptons. The shell of Bernie's seaside house was constructed from scratch on reserve land and torn down soon after filming. A free-for-all, no-idea-is-too-stupid-or-outrageous attitude pervaded the shooting. Want to staple Bernie's toupee to his head? Go for it. Toss him over the side of the balcony onto the sand? Why not? The rising tide washes him out to sea? Even better. And in another example of interaction with props saving the day, there was a scene in which I was sitting on the back deck with Bernie, looking out to sea. A pair of bikini-clad women were to walk past, call out, and wave. I was supposed to lift dead Bernie's arm to wave back. I felt as if I had little to do other than wait for the appropriate moment to fulfill a modest gag.

All through the filming I was staying in a condo that had a lot of board games on a shelf, and so on this day I brought Monopoly with me to work. I set up the board out on the deck, divvied up property, and played a very robust game with a very dead Bernie, even cheating him out of a little cash. The game not only gave me something to do, it illuminated character and enlivened a modest scene. It also spawned the even more ridiculous notion of rigging fishing line to Bernie's wrist so that when he was supposed to wave back, I simply had to pull on the string and my dead host could respond independently.

Ted, the director, often gave me free rein, and he responded to the idea. Ted was an explosive guy who occasionally lost his cool, screaming profanities through a bullhorn at scores of extras during a scene when we caught the ferry, or throwing the assistant director's walkie-talkie into the sea when it went off during a take. While his volatility was reminiscent of my father's, it was never directed at me, and his affectionate, confident persona reminded me of my brother Peter and made me feel safe. Ted was a gruff teddy bear. Near dawn, at the end of one all-night session, my costar Jonathan Silverman and I were struggling to find the humor in one scene, and after calling "Cut," Ted simply shouted, "Not funny!" as way of direction. He was right. We cut the scene. Ted also offered me my first chance to say "Action," directing him in a scene in which he played the cameo role of Jonathan's father. I'd never gotten to play comedy before, and the freedom it allowed and the precision it required appealed to me. The movie was a modest success, is still revered today among a certain type of fool (this one included), and spawned an ill-advised sequel about which nothing more will be said.

—

As the '80s were coming to an end, I was asked to go to Paris for the French auteur Claude Chabrol. He was adapting a little-known Henry Miller book titled *Quiet Days in Clichy* for the screen. He wanted me to play the lead, Miller himself. I had no idea how he came to me. I certainly had no presence in French cinema. It must have been an interesting series of meetings and conversations with any number of lists scoured, names considered and then reconsidered, until they settled on me for the job.

My lawyer, an old-time Hollywood power player, advised against the move. "People end their careers in Europe. They don't start them there."

And in some ways his words were prophetic. As the decade wore itself out, my brief tenure as a Hollywood heartthrob was coming to a close.

The self-exile was a welcome relief.

⟵

Along with Godard, Truffaut, and Eric Rohmer, Chabrol was a member of the French New Wave that came of age in the late 1950s. His films were often thrillers and displayed a master's touch of pure love for cinema.

Chabrol welcomed me—in a great many ways still a callow kid—into his sophisticated world and into his family. His stepdaughter, Cécile Maistre, who was also his assistant director, and I became close. His wife and script supervisor, Aurore, and I were fast chums. The four of us dined often. The only thing Chabrol loved more than filming was eating and talking about filming.

With the maestro, Chabrol.

Chabrol smoked a pipe and always smelled of sweet tobacco. He was small, roundish, and wore thick glasses. But the Mr. Magoo quality couldn't mask his genius. Chabrol's was the only movie set I ever went to when I wasn't working, simply to watch him create. We shot in Paris, Tuscany, and Rome.

Chabrol had a habit of answering my questions with affectionate French vagueness.

"Maestro"—he was always "Maestro"—"why do you want me to pick up the glass on that line?"

"My dear poor boy"—I was often "my dear poor boy"—"because I prefer."

He also gave me the single most effective direction I have ever received. One day we were doing a scene in a locker room and he suggested I give the other actor "a little whack with your towel."

I grumbled, "I don't know, Maestro."

He held up his hands as if in surrender. "My dear poor American boy, it is your part. I gave it to you. Ruin it if you want."

I whacked the actor with the towel.

French Films...

That Chabrol, a man I so respected and had so much affection for, saw me in a similar light went a long way to filling a paternal hole that I had come to accept without realizing its existence. I returned to Paris for years after filming *Jours tranquilles à Clichy* for an annual meal with Chabrol. When he died in 2010, Cécile sent me one of his ties—with a gravy stain on it, naturally.

My own father and I reconciled at the end of his life, in 2016. A few weeks after his divorce from my mother was final, he had met a woman in Las Vegas and they quickly married. My brother Peter told me about the wedding, since by then my father and I very rarely spoke. But my dad was wrong in assuming I wouldn't have attended the ceremony had I been invited. He moved to Maine, and I saw or heard from him only occasionally over the years. He remained married to Ursula, I believe happily, to the end.

They had escaped the Maine winter and rented a stranger's home in South Carolina when I got a call. My father's health had taken a turn. I went to see him as he was dying.

At his bedside, I told him I was sorry I had not been the son he had wanted. He said he was glad I came. Days later he was beyond talking. In death throes he lunged out at me, toward my throat. Instantly a child again, I jumped back in fear. Then, realizing he couldn't harm me anymore, I took his hand—cold, lizard-like now. I felt embarrassment, shame, but I didn't let go. I told him that I was there, that I was not going anywhere. I saw the fear in his eyes that I had seen my entire life but had been unable to name as fear until that moment. I said that it was okay. I told him he was safe now. He was free. He stared at me. Could he even see me anymore? Had he ever?

Ursula had placed an old boom box in the room. On it was a tape playing some of my father's favorite songs: Mahalia Jackson's version of "Amazing Grace," Kate Smith singing "God Bless America," and, from my youth, Trini Lopez swinging to "Lemon Tree." How many times as a child had I heard my dad—sometimes marching through the house naked after a shower, other times in his gray sweats and wool cap, just in from a jog, or maybe sitting at the kitchen table blowing blue smoke up into a shaft of sunlight, from one of his fat and pungent cigars, singing

Lemon tree, very pretty, and the lemon flower is sweet,
But the fruit of the lemon is impossible to eat.

Long stretches passed when there was no sign of life and I thought perhaps he was gone. Then would come a great heaving breath, his entire carriage rising, then collapsing back down into itself, and he would be still again. I began to count the time between breaths, forty-five, fifty seconds, a minute. Then would come another great and desperate gasp. My father would not go gently.

I sat. I realized I was privileged to be there.

We didn't right our wrongs, nor resolve our past, but simply put its burden down.

I began drinking again during the filming with Chabrol—as I invariably knew I would at some point. My initial pause had been based on simply depriving myself of something I desired; there had as yet been no wholesale change in attitude that is required to successfully step away from alcohol. We were shooting in Tuscany. I was in the small dressing caravan of my costar, a fabulous and posh Englishman named Nigel Havers. Nigel offered me a beer, Tuborg Gold in a can. I took it. As I raised it to my lips, my hand began to tremble; I knew, as Nigel could not have known, that I was putting a match to kerosene. His wife, Polly, noted my trembling hand. I laughed it off and took another swig.

I got away with my drinking during the rest of that filming, but it would continue to grow for the next three years, until the summer of 1992, when, at age twenty-nine, I would at last, as Henry Miller said, give up the ghost.

Those final three years of drinking were lost, painful years, to my career and to me personally. I drank my way through London and Cambridge doing a movie for the BBC, then squandered an opportunity on a film in Rome with John Frankenheimer. That I allowed him to bully and terrify me was no one's fault but my own—and not aided by the vast quantities of alcohol I was consuming.

Back in New York, I recall one morning much like the others. Violently hungover, racked by convulsions, I stumbled to the bathroom, only to see a small square of torn toilet paper lying on the floor. This proved my undoing; I dropped to my knees and sobbed at the disorder and chaos that my life had become.

Eventually, I hospitalized myself for a medical detox. Pumped full of Librium, I shuffled through the linoleum-tiled hallways with my ass hanging out of a paper robe, staring down at the large smiley faces imprinted on the toes of the foam slippers they provided me at check-in. My roommate was a drag queen who was in on vacation, happy to be off the street and enjoying "three hots and a cot." I liked her. After a week I was sent to rehab. I was recognized from the movies. Fellow inmates instantly took to calling me Zero because of *Less Than Zero*. I huddled under the covers of my single bed, convulsing in terror and shame. Mercifully, on the second day of my incarceration, I had a seizure in the lunch line—I had neglected to inform anyone that I was addicted to Xanax as well as alcohol—and was sent back to the hospital. Then, after a month in the country, I got myself straightened out and I began a life without alcohol or drugs that has continued, day in and day out.

For years afterward I feared that if I were to become successful in a very public way again I might return to drinking. The notion of success and drink had become somehow soldered together in my mind. Even after intellectually knowing that the two things were not related, it took decades to accept it in my bones.

Without my true emotions smothered beneath alcohol, I found it impossible to embrace what I had grown to understand was required of me for movieland success. Leaving home early one morning to catch a flight to Los Angeles, I turned to lock my door in gray predawn and suddenly heard myself say aloud a line from the twenty-third psalm: "Yea, though I walk through the valley of the shadow of death, I will fear no evil."

Overly dramatic to be sure, but as I wasn't a religious person and not aware that I even knew the psalm, my quoting it as I was about to fly off to the belly of the beast illuminated for me in that instant a reluctance about Hollywood that I couldn't shake. Sobriety hadn't altered that. For a number of years I would continue to strain forward, even as I made a hard retreat, compromising any progress I might make in a now-familiar push-pull emotional strain.

Early on in *The Great Gatsby*, F. Scott Fitzgerald describes the character Tom Buchanan as "a national figure in a way, one of those men who reach such an acute limited excellence at twenty-one that everything afterward savors of anticlimax." The eloquence of Fitzgerald's words does little to quell the somewhat chilling conclusion that it might not be unfair to similarly classify me. While I could do nothing to alter the perception of others, the trick—one it would take me some time to discover—would be to move past that ensuing anticlimax in *my own* estimation, to avoid what Fitzgerald famously proclaimed elsewhere when he wrote, "There are no second acts in American lives."

Fortunately, I was to make an unlikely discovery.

On a whim, in the mid-1990s, I walked across Spain for five hundred miles on the Camino de Santiago, an ancient pilgrimage trail. The solitary trip changed my life; fear—the kind I had seen in my father's eyes on his deathbed—had so infused my own experience and was revealed to me for the first time. That journey set in motion long and often solitary periods of wanderlust that led to my writing about travel. Over the next fifteen years I became associated with magazines and newspapers for my travel writing, found success in it, extracted deep satisfaction from it, and discovered the same emotional reservoir within myself that I had found when I first began acting. Only this time I did things on my terms, controlling what outlets I wrote for and what I produced that would be presented to the world. No one was going to brand me this time but me. At the same time I found myself yearning for life on the filmmaking sets I had come of age on—sets that had excited me and continued to do so. I began directing for television. My early interest in the more complete aspects of filmmaking beyond acting finally had a place to be applied. Directing afforded me protection from the glare of being in front of the camera while allowing me to employ all I had learned over the years. The conflicting impulses I had always experienced were relieved and I could simply go to work without holding back.

Yet acting remained, a shadow hovering over me and informing who I was—even as it does now. Acting was how I had first located myself. The sheer span of time during which I pursued it, the challenges and confusion it put me through, the personality changes it had demanded from me, the satisfactions and joys it had provided me, the life it had afforded and defined for me—none of it can be discarded. Ultimately, it is not only what I am but who I am. I long ago stopped yearning for the kind of career that I was never going to have, although the simplicity with which I once viewed acting occasionally slips in and fills me with an echo of that yearning, not so much for the fame or recognition but for the purity of that early desire and its feeling of aliveness.

A number of years ago I wrote a travel memoir and was making the rounds doing publicity. I found myself on Alec Baldwin's podcast *Here's the Thing*. I didn't know Alec but found him an engaged and curious interviewer. At one point we were talking about my youthful success and I mentioned, in perhaps a self-flagellating way, how I had pulled back when I was at my most public. To which Alec said simply, "Maybe you didn't want it."

His comment stopped me in my tracks. Up until that moment I had never actively considered such a thing. I had always assumed my habitual apprehension to be simply my failing. After all, who wouldn't want fame? Movie stars are the royalty of our culture, adored and pampered. On reflection

I could see that Alec's observation was only half-correct—ambivalence is always more complex—but in the simplicity of his comment, he had come closer to the core of it than I ever had. I wanted to be successful, to excel at what I did, to be recognized for it. My self-esteem craved it, my ego welcomed the gratification, and my insecurities were at least superficially pacified. Yet by temperament I was in many ways ill-suited for such a public life, especially at a young age when I had yet to carve out who I was within myself. Well documented to be a perilous ledge, fame is not the ground on which to find one's footing. And I had intuitively recognized that the disproportionate attention associated with fame was not necessarily in my best interests. A very real part of me simply didn't want my experience dominated by it. But that was what had happened for a time.

What makes all that more complex is that in a great many ways acting saved my life. When I stepped onstage as the Artful Dodger all those years ago, a light went on inside me that has never gone out. I came close to extinguishing it through alcohol, but my subsequent recovery, like a crucible, has only changed its form and added another hue to its flame. And yet, among a certain generation of people, the work I did as a young man will forever burn brightest. And it's not just the work: maybe now, more importantly, it is the *memory* of the work that's so valuable to people. Because in the memory of those movies exists a touchstone of youth, of when life was all ahead, when the future was a blank slate, when anything was possible.

How did I get here?

When I received that first call from Chabrol, I am embarrassed to say I had never heard of him. For advice, I called on my friend Ken Kwapis, who had directed me back at the beginning, in *The Beniker Gang*. There were others whom I might have called, others with whom I spoke more often, with whom I was closer, but for some reason I called Ken. I trusted him. He had *seen* me at the start and was among the first to believe in me. I asked if he had any idea who this Frenchman named Chabrol was. "Are you kidding?" Ken said. "Get on a plane and go. Don't ask questions."

During my initial phone call with Chabrol, I asked him if he thought it was a good idea for me, at twenty-six, to play

Miller, who was in his mid-forties during the events in the book. The very Chabrolian response he offered made no sense to me at the time, but over the years I have begun to see its wisdom. Over a scratchy line, in his thick French accent, the Maestro assured me, "My dear poor boy, the truth today is not the truth tomorrow."

Chabrol might just as easily have been speaking about the Brat Pack itself. The open secret, of course, is that the Brat Pack, at least in my experience, never really existed at all—not in a physical sense anyway. That I've never again seen Judd Nelson or Emilio Estevez since the day we finished *St. Elmo's Fire*, and that I have run into the others only sporadically over the years— nor have I even met many of my Brat Pack brethren—speaks loudly only to my own extreme sense of singularity rather than any misgivings about the group or any of its members.

Had the Brat Pack existed as a tight-knit community, perhaps we might have found a way to band together and withstand the stinging comments from a disparaging media— maybe even been able to laugh it off. Instead, a cluster of young and scared actors trying to make a name for themselves got some mud slung at them and ran for the hills.

It would take time for me to not feel that I had been side-swiped by the tag and then shackled to it. To label anything so easily is to make no further attempt at understanding it. Yet that label also elevated me even as it weighed me down. It gave me stature while diminishing me, made me a part of something even as it isolated me, gave me a platform and limited my options.

Some other members of the Brat Pack might contest my

assertion, but the power of the group label ultimately enlarged all of our statures as it solidified us in the minds of the public. That idea of camaraderie, even if it was just an idea—of shared experience, of being a part of something greater, of being among the ultimate in-crowd, particularly in youth—is something for which many of us yearn.

While originally cast in disparaging judgment, the Brat Pack label has grown over the years to radiate a warm nostalgia for a time of youth recalled through rose-colored lenses. It was a stigma that ultimately transformed into a loving moniker, a term of great and enduring affection, even as a shadow of its early taint lingered. It has become both a thing and its opposite—harsh rebuke and sweet affection coexisting.

What there is no doubt about is that those '80s movies themselves touched something deep in a generation of moviegoers. *Pretty in Pink* et al. helped so many to feel like they mattered, helped them to feel seen, less misunderstood, less alone. And those films continue to live on. The fact that people are still compelled to share their appreciation with me keeps those films alive in me as well, despite my occasional protestations that they reside firmly in my past. That appreciation has helped to melt away any lingering resistance I've felt over the years to the Brat Pack label. For that, I'm grateful. As a person who has long wrestled with the push-pull of connection versus separation, those films have placed me firmly in the world and among my generation in a way that is both singular and communal. What better place could I hope to land? And a term that has carried as many contradictions as the Brat Pack has, and has existed in the extremes of passion over so long a period of time, is ultimately something worth embracing.

If the 1980s began for me in and around Washington Square Park, they ended on the streets of Berlin. Chabrol asked me to do a second film with him, in Germany. While we shot, the world reimagined itself around us. Filming by day and celebrating on the street at night, I lost myself among tense, wildly exultant crowds as the Berlin Wall fell in November of 1989.

I was among the hordes surging down by the wall, not far from Checkpoint Charlie, where I had crossed into East Berlin for an afternoon visit with the Chabrols just a few days earlier. Cheered on by the crowd, a man beside me swung a large sledgehammer at the wall. The night was biting cold, and steam shot out from his nostrils as he heaved. Chunks of the wall fell free and I retrieved one from the ground. A hand reached out, grabbed me, and spun me around. A German soldier stared down at me.

"You," he said in English. My arm still in his grasp.

I dropped my piece of the wall.

"I'm sorry," I blurted.

"Come." He dragged me through the crowd a short distance, until a small folding table came into view. On it were paper cups filled with steaming hot chocolate. He shoved one into my hand.

"*Catholic Boys*," he said.

Confused, I shouted to be heard over the crowd: "What?"

"*Catholic Boys*, za film."

Heaven Help Us, the second movie I had ever done, was called by its original working title, *Catholic Boys,* in Europe—where, unlike in the US, it had been a big hit.

Relieved, I grabbed back at the soldier. "Yes!" I shouted.

Smiling broadly now, nodding his head and pumping my hand up and down, he said simply, "Good. Good."

He then turned me by my shoulders and shoved me back into the heaving throng.

I dove into the night and was swept along. Just as I had been swept along through so much since first arriving in New York a decade earlier, a scared, dreaming seventeen-year-old kid. The city had embraced me, success had befallen me, and my life would never be the same. I would be altered, confused, scarred, and ultimately completed and made whole by that experience.

As Berlin roiled in rejuvenation around me now, I pulsed with the crowds, grabbing up another piece of the crumbling Berlin Wall. Eventually I made my way back toward my hotel late at night when the streets were cold and quiet. I walked and walked, a stranger far from home at home in myself. Still warm from the excitement, my breath visible with each exhalation, I was grateful to have been there for all of it, in the right place at the right time.

I live today, as I have for almost all of the nearly forty years I've been in New York, in the West Village. I'm just a few blocks from the small, third-story, one-bedroom apartment with the sloping floors and faulty fireplace that I lived in

At five. Bring it on.

during so much of my early success. I pass the building on a near-daily basis. Occasionally I glance up.

Late last spring, as I was walking through the neighborhood, on Tenth Street I saw a familiar figure up ahead. She was more stooped and, even at a distance, frailer than the last time I'd seen her more than a decade earlier. Back then she had come to a play I was appearing in. My old teacher hadn't cared for the play or my work in it, and in her usual fashion she had not been shy in telling me so. Yet she had still shown up, still put in the time for me, just as she had when I first got up in front of her class to do a sound exercise and couldn't stand still.

Now Terry was being assisted by what clearly was an aide worker.

Terry Hayden, my first acting teacher, who had believed in me so many years ago when no one else had—who had taught me and given me a way to think about acting and a reverence for it—was being helped down the few stairs into her garden apartment. I had passed Terry's place countless times over the years and always looked in the window to make sure her dream catcher was still hanging from the latch and that her small animal figurines were still on the dusty windowsill.

Terry would die in a few short months. I, of course, could not know this at the time. I stopped and watched her vanish inside, along with her caregiver. They left the gate open and I considered going to close it behind them.

Then the aide worker came back out to secure the door. I hurried up to her and spoke through the wire mesh. I was an old student of Terry's, I explained. Could I possibly pay my respects? The aide worker looked at me with exhausted eyes, and at last she spoke.

"Hang on." She disappeared inside. I waited. My heart beat quickly, just as it had years ago as I waited for the doorman to allow me up during that early audition for *Class*, wondering if it had all been some kind of mistake.

The caregiver returned. "You can come in."

I bent down to get through the door under the stoop and turned right into the cluttered apartment. It seemed little had changed in the more than thirty years since I was last inside her place. Terry sat in a low chair facing the door, across the small room. There was a single path through the accumulation of ninety-eight years of life to her chair. Her eyes were on me the entire way. Watery, questioning.

I could see that Terry didn't recognize me anymore. To be

at eye level, I got on my knees before her. I told her who I was and that I had come to thank her: Everything I have, everything I became, none of it would have been possible without you. Because of you, because of what you taught me, because of the belief you showed in me, because of what you saw in me, long before I could see it myself. I owe so much to you. And I need to tell you that.

Terry listened and then grabbed at my fingers with her trembling hands.

"And now you have gotten on your knees and repaid that debt," she said, her voice quivering hard. Then she flung her hand out, as if gesturing to the balcony, or sowing seeds. "Now, go. Go!"

I stood, feeling I had received a sacred blessing.

Acknowledgments

It's been a long and uneven path to produce this book. It was almost written thirty years ago, and then a few times after that (I'm glad it wasn't). The notion surfaced again when Jonathan Karp asked me to consider it at a moment when I was willing to hear the idea—so my gratitude goes to him. My deep thanks and appreciation to Michael Oats Palmer, who read an early draft and offered invaluable insights and direction. And to Dan Wilhelm, who read *two* early versions (now that's a friend). Sara Switzer gave insightful feedback, as did Joanne Steglitz. David Patterson is owed a great debt. David Kuhn shepherded the manuscript through with his usual care, candor, and insight, with valuable assistance from Nate Mancusso.

The folks at Grand Central could not have been more supportive. Thank you to both Ben Sevier and Karen Kosztolnyik. My editor, Suzanne O'Neill, was an early and constant cheerleader as well as a velvet-fisted taskmaster, asking for more, and then asking again. The book is richer because of her, and she deserves my very real gratitude. Thanks go to David Chesanow for his delicate copyedit. Liz Connor captured so much of whom I wanted to be in my youth with her beautiful cover art, and Marie Mundaca's grace with the interior design illuminated how I would like it presented today. Thank you to Jeff Holt, my meticulous production editor. Matthew Ballast and Kamrun Nesa have worked tirelessly in publicity, as have Amanda Pritzker and Alana Spendley in marketing. And Jacqueline Young kept all the trains running—thank you.

Huge thanks need to be directed at Brian Liebman for his ongoing support and belief. Jill Fritzo is more levelheaded than anyone I know—deep and ongoing thanks to her and her team: Michael Geiser, Stephen Fertelmes, Charlie Roina, and Kelly Dickau. Thanks to social media–savvy Katrina Poulos.

Thank you, Keith Bellows. I miss you.

Thank you to Sam, Willow, and Rowan, who laugh at pictures of the kid in this book and who couldn't really care all that much about stuff that happened so long ago.

And ultimately, to Dolores, who raises the bar on everything.

PHOTO CREDITS

Courtesy of Greg Gorman page iv

Courtesy of MTV / ViacomCBS page 3

CLASS © 1983 Orion Pictures Corporation. All Rights Reserved. Courtesy of Metro-Goldwyn-Mayer Studios Inc. page 89

CLASS © 1983 Orion Pictures Corporation. All Rights Reserved. Courtesy of Metro-Goldwyn-Mayer Studios Inc. page 94

Courtesy of Ken Kwapis page 114

AF Archive / Alamy Stock Photo page 120

Eric Edwards, Courtesy of Sundance Institute page 127

ZUMA Press, Inc. / Alamy Stock Photo page 134

Getty Images / Time & Life Pictures page 137

Photo by Martha Swope © The New York Public Library for the Performing Arts page 161

New York Magazine and Box Media, LLC, Photographer Greg Gorman page 166

PictureLux / The Hollywood Archive / Alamy Stock Photo page 169

Photo 12 / Alamy Stock Photo page 176

Getty Images / Terry O'Neill page 180

TCD/Prod.DB / Alamy Stock Photo page 188

Alamy page 189

RGR Collection / Alamy Stock Photo page 202

United Archives GmbH / Alamy Stock Photo page 210

About the Author

ANDREW MCCARTHY is the author of two previous books, *The Longest Way Home* (a travel memoir) and *Just Fly Away* (a young-adult novel)—both *New York Times* bestsellers. He is an award-winning travel writer, a television director, and an actor, having appeared on-screen for nearly four decades in such films as *Pretty in Pink*, *St. Elmo's Fire*, and *Less Than Zero*.